APHRODITE AND THE OTHERS

Gillian Bouras was born in Melbourne in 1945. She worked as a teacher in Australia before moving to Greece with her husband and children in 1980. Her first book about this experience was *A Foreign Wife*, published in 1986, and this was followed by *A Fair Exchange* in 1991. Gillian is a contributor to various newspapers, magazines and journals, both in Australia and overseas.

BY THE SAME AUTHOR

A Foreign Wife
A Fair Exchange

APHRODITE
and the
OTHERS

GILLIAN BOURAS

McPHEE GRIBBLE PUBLISHERS

McPhee Gribble
Penguin Books Australia Ltd
487 Maroondah Highway, PO Box 257
Ringwood, Victoria 3134, Australia
Penguin Books Ltd
Hardmondsworth, Middlesex, England
Viking Penguin, A Division of Penguin Books USA Inc
375 Hudson Street, New York, New York 10014, USA
Penguin Books Canada Limited
10 Alcorn Avenue, Toronto, Ontario, Canada M4V 3B2
Penguin Books (NZ) Ltd
182–190 Wairau Road, Auckland 10, New Zealand

First published by McPhee Gribble 1994
1 3 5 7 9 10 8 6 4 2
Copyright © Gillian Bouras, 1994

Produced by McPhee Gribble
56 Claremont Street, South Yarra, Victoria 3141, Australia
A division of Penguin Books Australia Ltd

Designed by Catherine Howarth
Typeset in 11½/13pt Berner by Midland Typesetters
Printed in Australia by Australian Print Group

National Library of Australia
Cataloguing-in-Publication data:

Bouras, Gillian, 1945–   .
Aphrodite and the others.
ISBN 0 86914 316 6.
1. Bouras, Aphrodite. 2. Peloponnesus (Greece)–Social conditions.
I. Title.
949.52

*For Aphrodite, whether she likes it or not,
and for the three men in a castle.*

ACKNOWLEDGEMENTS

The author is grateful for the award of a Hawthornden Fellowship during April and May 1992. Without the tranquillity of a stay at Hawthornden Castle International Retreat for Writers, this book would not have been written.

The author also thanks Dr G. M. Dow and Mr M. C. Jones for their help, friendship and support.

Part of chapter two of this book was first published in the autumn 1990 edition of *Island* magazine.

Duke: And what's her history?
Viola: A blank, my lord.

Twelfth Night, *Act II, Scene iv*

History is a string full of knots;
the best you can do is admire it,
and maybe knot it up a bit more.

Jeanette Winterson

APHRODITE'S FAMILY

George Bouras
(A common ancestor who fled to Asia Minor and
then fled back to Stamatinou towards the end of the 18th century.)

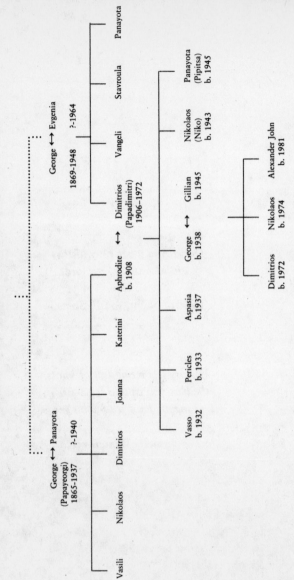

NOTE: Aphrodite did not change her name when she married. She and her husband, Dimitrios, were third cousins.

INTRODUCTION

Two women: Aphrodite and Gillian, who are also Yiayia and my self. Of course that is not the whole story, for many other people are involved in the plot. But for what seems like an eternity, and is in fact at least twelve years, everything came back to Yiayia and me, to the tensions between us, to the fact that we loved the same people, to the fact that we resented each other deeply, to her certainties, to my uncertainties, to our irreconcilable differences. Chalk and cheese. She and I. She secure in her place and in her culture, I the displaced person trying, not very successfully, to maintain contact with my own background, my spiritual home.

It seemed to me that I had to make all the effort, and that is not the whole story either. Of course not, for things are never that simple. But if I pretend that they are simple enough, then the story is one of both triumph and defeat. Hers is the triumph: she is the great survivor. Eighty-six this year, she has survived poverty, war and famine, dire hardship and continuous work, constant childbirth and the occasional threat of death. And mine is the defeat, for, try as I might, and I did try, I could not be what she and others wanted, could not become what her world demanded as a right. The moral? In the end, we can only be, any of us, what we are. Yiayia knows who and what she is, has never had any doubts. As for myself, I am none too sure who and what I am, and never have been sure.

Aphrodite/Yiayia: Greek. Traditional woman. Daughter of a Greek Orthodox priest. Wife of a Greek Orthodox priest, Papadimitri. Mother of six living children: Vasso, Pericles, Aspasia, George, Niko and Pipitsa. Grandmother, *yiayia*, of two granddaughters and eleven grandsons, three of whom are half Australian, half Greek. Great-grandmother of two little girls: Katerina Aphrodite and Vassiliki. Mother-in-law, the *pethera*, of Gillian. She is illiterate; although she once knew how to write her name, she has now forgotten.

Gillian/my self: Australian. Definitely Australian. I feel certain of this, at least, although my eldest son, who now lives in Australia, says I am not Australian any more, for I have been away too long. I have been away since 1980, the year I moved to a Peloponnesian village. Ancestry English, Scots, Irish. A teacher. Daughter and granddaughter of teachers. Wife of Yiayia's fourth and favourite child, George. Mother of three sons: Dimitrios, aged twenty-one; Nikolaos, nineteen; and Alexander, the only Greek-born one, who is twelve. I am literate, obviously, but ignorant of almost everything Yiayia thinks important. I am the daughter-in-law, the *nifi*, of Aphrodite.

Biographies are usually formal structures, edifices erected on a framework of facts, buttressed by footnotes, with stress factors checked and estimated, allowed for, taken into account. For every biography there are usually whole shelves of secondary sources, files of primary sources in crabbed handwriting, bundles of letters tied with ribbon and string, and the usual detritus of a life: certification of births, marriages, deaths; tax returns, files marked 'Documents, Personal'.

This biography does not fit that pattern, for Yiayia has no books, no files. She has only her identity card and her health book, which entitles her to medical benefits and rebates at the chemist's shop. She receives no letters, can have no idea of the sheer pleasure of correspondence, has no notion of Jane Austen's definition of letters as being 'thorough pictures of the heart'. Writing about her life has necessitated, in a sense, a jolting and often unsatisfactory return to prehistory: the environment, the dwellings, and even the artifacts have had to be hard evidence.

But there are also the voices. It is the poet's business and also the biographer's, surely, to write down the voices, to shape history and personality from the vibrations, to try at least to do these things. The achievement of these aims is a different matter altogether.

To people who live in an oral society it is the voice, obviously, which has primary importance, and hearing and listening have a different value from the one they have for literate people. The logic of this is obvious, for are not voices as individual as fingerprints? And it is surely no accident, not a mere coincidence, that most rural Greeks are very talented mimics. Now, in the 1990s, oral people must have noise. Television sets and radios babble away in the background, replacing, to some extent, the noise of families working in the olive groves, replicating the hum and buzz in the square and *kafeneion*.

It is Yiayia's voice in particular that I try to write down. 'How did you get your name?' I ask.

'From my godmother, of course.' She is always more than slightly impatient when I ask what seem to her to be obvious questions. For years I have reacted badly to this apparent prickliness, gritting my teeth and counting to ten against what seems to me to be a form of verbal aggression. But I have learned the rules: never let your oral guard down, never give an inch. My problem is that I am not very good at the game.

But in this business of her name she naturally does not see my point, and how can I explain that I have always thought it slightly odd that a priest's daughter should be called Aphrodite? (And now it seems to me that the names Penelope or Ariadne would have been choices just as appropriate.) Yiayia's brothers and sisters were all named after Orthodox saints, and the Church, at least now, prefers these: a Greek-Australian couple of my acquaintance had difficulty in finding an Orthodox priest who would baptise their child Marilyn.

Once I thought the name Aphrodite a terrible burden, and dreaded the thought that I would have to give it to a daughter. English speakers mispronounce it: in Greek it is lighter, sweeter, as befits one who arose from the foam and caused flowers and grasses to grow wherever she trod.

'But why Aphrodite?' I persist.

'That was my godmother's own name, and as a god-

4

parent can give a child any name he or she wants, she gave me hers. She was a good woman, a beautiful woman. She was our neighbour, who left and went to America. But she came back and named me.' And she sighs as she usually does when she thinks of America. America to her means, above all, the brother who is not even a shadowy memory, the Nikolaos who went to Chicago and never returned.

But as most people use her title, her name is virtually lost. Occasionally, however, I make a point of using it. For, like Byron, who mentioned 'the glory and the nothing of a name', I believe that a name has at least some power, and that of Aphrodite more than most, for this was the name of the goddess of beauty, fertility and love, a very ancient deity, a force of nature whom it could be dangerous to deny.

'Allow me to introduce my mother-in-law, Kyria Aphrodite,' I say to visitors, and she grins wryly, pleased at hearing her name, displeased at my wilful omission of her title: *Papathia*, priest's wife. Of such actions and reactions is our relationship composed.

It has been said that, as the singer sang the epos, so the writer spins the story as part of his self. The twentieth-century citizen, according to Illich and Sanders, authors of *ABC: The Alphabetization of the Popular Mind*, 'sees himself through the eyes of various sciences as a layer cake of texts'. For the literate person the self is created out of confessions, journals, diaries, memories and autobiography.

So Aphrodite and I are divided by almost every conceivable factor, gap and chasm: country, culture, age, education, language, and finally by the concept of self. For an oral person the 'I' can exist most fully and truly in the actual act of speaking aloud. Things are not as simple, or, one is tempted to add, as genuine or pure for the literate person.

The claims made on the oral self are many: home and

workplace demand constant and total devotion to the task, the state demands patriotism, the Church unquestioning piety. Oral people are not, usually, self-analytical. They cannot see themselves, obviously, as a 'layer cake of texts'. Their sense of self most often comes through the evaluation of outsiders. They are what other people say.

In an anthology used by Greek children in the first year of high school there is a story about an illiterate shepherd and his wife who unwittingly play host to St Basil on New Year's Eve. The connection between illiteracy on the one hand and purity and simplicity on the other is very strongly suggested. The shepherd says, «Εγώ αγαπώ πολύ τα γράμματα της θρησκείας μας, κι ας μην τα καταλαβαίνω, γιατι είμαι ξύλο απελέκητο.» 'I love the writings of our religion, even if I don't understand them, uncarved wood that I am.' Here is the difference between sound and sight. The question the oral person asks is Zorba's question, «Τι λένε τα κιτάπια;» 'What do the notebooks say?'

Yiayia does not call me by my proper name: I am the only adult who calls her Yiayia. And even in this act, our ideas of self are modified. Her self is not merely a yiayia; my self is very definitely not a Julie or a Yorgina. They are running on parallel tracks, these selves, or unravelling separate strings from lintels set far apart, and are destined never to meet.

Even now, after all this time, she and I often sit and ponder, each struggling to follow the other's thought processes. She cannot set mine down, even if she wanted to. But I wish to preserve hers, even though I do not claim to understand them. Why do I wish this? Why have I tried to write something about a woman who cannot read, and who would not want to read what I write even if she could? She chuckles about my writing; why would anyone want to do it? But she does, I suspect, have a sneaking regard

6

for *ta grammata*, the letters, does at least feel a little jealousy of those who can read.

The dilemma of the biographer seems particularly trying in this case. I have undoubtedly brought my own prejudices and perceptions to bear on the story of my mother-in-law's life. I am too introspective, too analytical, too Western, too middle class to have written about a woman who had no choices in life, who simply had to take what it handed her, who had the pattern of her life set even before her birth. But the fact remains that I wanted to make this attempt to meet a life which has made little attempt to meet mine.

I wanted to set down the story, to capture a taste of the flavour before it is too late; to catch, as Anaïs Nin said, the life which is flowing away from us every minute. I wanted to make a gesture. This has been, in a sense, a labour of love. And now I look at the word and feel timid about using it. Love is not a word I have ever used to described the relationship between Yiayia and myself. We have given each other a hard time, she and I. Neither was what the other expected; we have, on occasion, shocked and hurt each other.

I do not know what I have ever done for Yiayia, except that I have made her laugh often. That much is certain, for she is, I think, fairly convinced that I am mad: eccentric at best, insane at worst. More often she has shaken her head. But there is always the value of novelty: I can still surprise her. I do know what she has done for me, even while trying my limited amount of patience sorely. She has shown me another world and extended the boundaries of my own received life. It is an irony that her own small world has made mine larger, that her acceptance of her life's patterns has made me question and redraw the lines and grids of my own, that her oral world has made me more aware of both the privilege and the poverty there is in being literate.

7

She has given me, strange though it may seem, a link to my own past. It is now easier to imagine the lives my great-great-grandmothers lived: the rural round, no matter which hemisphere they inhabited; the agony and danger of almost constant childbirth; the threat of drought, famine, poverty and death; the sense of being totally dependent on a man, and on his good nature; the general sense of powerlessness. No wonder she and they liked to exercise power the only way available, within the home.

Picture my paternal grandfather's mother, married at seventeen, pregnant for the first time at eighteen and for the last time at forty-three. On the last occasion her doctor suggests a hot bath and liberal doses of gin, but she is too frightened to try this time-honoured solution to her pressing problem. See my grandfather, aged twenty-three, fighting for king and country in Flanders Fields, receiving news of the arrival of a baby sister. He has already lost his favourite sister to diphtheria; another, younger sister dies after eating a toadstool; a dog saves another child from drowning in the home dam. Seven of twelve children survive to adulthood, and the baby born last is one of the first to die.

Consider, as well, Yiayia's mother Panayota, climbing olive trees during the harvest every year because her priest husband couldn't or wouldn't do it.

'What? Long skirts and all?'

'*Mallista*. Certainly, long skirts and all. *Ach, i kakomira*, the ill-fated one.'

So now I sit and write and think not only of Aphrodite but of Panayota, Evgenia and all the other faceless, nameless Peloponnesian women, and of Eliza Jane and Harriet and the rest, whose blood, like so many little tributaries, runs in the veins of my sons. I think, too, of how the old women here in the village teach a lesson: that of how to resist the personal erosion that threatens as a result of continuous hard work; and I think of how, at their best, they provide some sort of balance to the solitary striving that is one of the main features of industrialized society. For they soak up existence; they are not programmed. Routine and the abstract have little meaning for them.

In May 1992 I was seated in the National Library of Scotland, struggling for what seemed like the best part of a day with the catalogue: all additions from 1978 were on computer. Green letters and figures leapt onto the screen and conveyed virtually nothing. Another press of the button elicited the suggestion that I enter the command HELP. Command? A cry in the jungle night seemed more like it. I managed one more step and then got completely bogged down in a vain effort to extract a shelf number. Pride in pocket, I asked for assistance. A stern twenty-year-old female came to my aid and was totally unmoved, as well she might be, by my blitherings about living in a Greek village. She would have been, like other people I have met recently, incredulous at the thought that I have never seen a fax machine. She did, however, provide me with the shelf number and with a few hints as well. The book I wanted and eventually procured was W. J. Ong's *Orality and Literacy: The Technologizing of the Word*.

Suddenly the complete irony of the situation struck me and I found it difficult to suppress rising hysteria. For months I had been using my own tools to shape a world I now know I can never live in, had been trying to make sense of the years spent feeling isolated because I have *ta grammata*, and because *ta grammata* I have are not the right ones. There I was, struggling to write a biography of an illiterate person and becoming daily more aware of the contradictions involved in the task. In the library a salutary lesson was taught me, for I, too, am an illiterate in the world where computer literacy is spreading its tentacles, just as much a dinosaur as Yiayia is in the world of the book.

The world of the book has always provoked divergent responses. In the *Phaedrus*, Plato made Socrates say that writing is inhuman, pretending to establish outside the mind what in reality can be only in the mind. It is a thing, a manufactured product, which destroys memory and weakens the faculties. Charlemagne, however, slept with a tablet under his pillow so that he could practise reading the alphabet whenever he awoke.

When an oral person becomes literate, he sacrifices a great deal, including a certain connection with the natural world. That sacrifice is a kind of death, as literacy is a new kind of life. Perhaps notions of both death and life fuse in the tale of Erasmus, as told by George Steiner:

Erasmus, walking home on a foul night, glimpsed a tiny fragment of print in the mire. He bent down, seized upon it and lifted it to a flickering light with a cry of thankful joy. Here was a miracle!

Stories, whether sung, told or written, are an enchantment that enables sorrow and suffering to be borne.

I have tried to tell the story.

CHAPTER ONE
A BEGINNING

*Woman was born to be the connecting link
between man and his human self, between
abstract ideas and the personal pattern which
creates them.*
The Diary of Anaïs Nin, *Anaïs Nin*

Once upon a time there lived a woman who had no mirrors in her house. When she did her long grey hair, threading and plaiting, tucking and weaving, she did it, most often, by feeling. Sometimes she looked in a window, but usually the windows were open so that she could look out on others, not in on herself. Or else she looked at her image as it was reflected in the water in the large copper basin which sat outside in the yard, beneath the tap that dripped occasionally but regularly, measuring time in its own way. Such water threw back ripples, wrinkles and corrugations.

Naturally, because she had no mirrors and no clear idea of what she looked like, she did not talk to her mirror self. She talked to the self within her, and sound was more important than sight, for sound links things, ideas, facts, memories, information together, producing harmony. Sight focusses on the singular, the disparate, the discrete: the lock of hair falling out of place, the smudge of soot on the nose, frown marks not quite matching above it. When you talk, you both create and hear yourself, hear and create, with the two processes operating simultaneously to form the power of I, weaving in and out, over and under.

In any case, a Greek village woman sees herself reflected in other women. They all look the same: headscarves, shapeless dresses, black stockings held at the knee by white elastic garters joined together with rough stitching. Black aprons, black cardigans. There is no need for mirrors. What, really, is the point of them?

But one day, quite unexpectedly, another woman arrives, joins the household, and stays. And stays. The first woman watches her and sees no reflection. The second woman is younger, she wears strange clothes: brief sleeveless cottons in summer, trousers and tops in winter. Woman, man, and back again – or at least that is the way it seems, and it is all very bewildering.

This woman does not talk, or talks only in a certain manner. Sometimes she does not talk at all, but makes noises which make no sense. She cannot speak very well to the first woman; she does not have the gift, is not talented in that way. She knows no riddles or rhymes, is ignorant of proverbs and spells, cannot make jokes.

She wants a mirror, and manages to ask if there is a full-length one in the house. There isn't, of course. That has already been said. She peers into a little round glass, part of something that is called, the first woman discovers, a compact. She mutters to herself, and pokes at her face, smoothes her hair.

Eventually she starts to talk, to say things, some of which are unexpected. What thoughts she has in her head. And what words. Her favourites are questions: Why? What? When? And the answers the first woman gives are, Because that's just the way it is, I told you, and, Why is it so important anyway?

Even after she learns to talk, this second woman is often silent, watching and gazing, looking at who can guess what. And at times like these, she does not seem to listen to anything or anybody, but makes squiggles and lines, notes in a little book. Who knows what becomes of all this?

This second woman cannot spin, weave, knit or crochet, or so it would appear, for she never does any of these things. She cannot make knots or put a pannier on the donkey; she tethers the donkey and he pulls free to wander the lanes because she has tied the rope the wrong way. She knows nothing. She does not understand how important rope is. She has not the least idea of the basic importance of knots.

In Greece rope and knots are very important: much can depend on the strength of a tether and on the ability to tie knots that do not slip. Rope is sold by weight and it is sold by grocers and ironmongers who stand coiling it into the pan of the scales, watching the needle swing. The thread of time, the weight of history.

It has been said that all history is the history of thought. It can also be argued that much history is the history of migration, for there have always been journeys. Indeed, the Greek poet George Seferis stated that « το πρώτο πράγμα που έκανε ο Θεός είναι το μακρινό ταξίδι. » 'The first thing that God made was the long journey.' And throughout history there have always been at least three types of people: those who wanted to travel; those who had journeys forced upon them; and those, who seem often to have been in the minority, who chose to stay in one place and were able to do so.

The development of both Australia and Greece would have been vastly different without the fact of the journey, the voyage, the trek. In my family, we like to think that Captain Cook's lieutenant, Zachary Hicks, who first shouted, 'Land ho!' at six o'clock in the morning on 20 April 1770, on sighting the promontory that later bore his name, was a remote ancestor. It is almost certainly not true.

What is true is that Catherine the Great of Russia had been forced, because of the Russo-Turkish war, to look just slightly south at about the same time: one of her many favourites supported an uprising against the Turks in the Morea, that part of the Ottoman empire now known as the Peloponnese. In the history of Aphrodite's village the facts are these: the Orlov rebellion of 1769 failed and the villagers, like all others in the Peloponnese, were powerless against the Albanians, brought in by the Turks, who killed and kidnapped those people who would not give up their Orthodox faith. Some villagers did indeed manage to survive by living quietly in their mountain fastnesses. Others fled.

George Bouras was one of those who left. The story is that at the end of the eighteenth century he became a shepherd for an aga in Asia Minor and thus managed to live comfortably, eventually building up a considerable fortune. The string of his personal history seemed to be unravelling quietly and satisfactorily enough until the night his son Dimitrios went to steal fruit in a Turkish orchard.

This story has been handed down by word of mouth,

along a generations-long thread of sound. There is no mirror of text to show us the reflection of the past, to allow us to see the dark glimmer of motivation. Dimitrios, stealing fruit (surely he did not need to do this?) in the orchard, is surprised by a Turk. Overcome by panic, Dimitrios kills him. George Bouras panics in his turn; by morning the whole family, which includes at least five sons, has fled, leaving everything behind.

A boat takes them from the shores of Asia Minor to those of Messinian Bay in the Peloponnese, but the length of the journey is not recorded and we know nothing of the weather, or of the fear these people must have been feeling. The Turkish chapter is closed; they are about to start new lives in their old home. But it is not as simple as that. George Bouras is unable to pay the passage money. An agreement is reached: three of his children remain on board as hostages until he and the rest can produce the requisite sum.

And once again we know some facts and are ignorant of others. The rest of the family somehow makes its way inland, up and over mountains until they come to the second of the ancestral villages. What we do not know is how long the three children have to wait for their father to return; we are not sure how he raises the money, but raise the money he does, and now the children are free. We have no idea whether they are male or female, and there is no reflection of their mother, no dazzle, blink or glow. Nothing. In that time, in that part of the world, men made history, women produced the men and then were heard and seen no more.

The generations which follow see the War of Independence and the establishment of the modern Greek state. For the locals, some events are more important than others. In 1821 village men take part in the assault on beleaguered Turks at Tripolis. In 1825 Ibrahim Pasha lands at Methoni and lays waste the land for miles around. (Most of the olive trees in today's village were planted after this time, the originals having been burned by Ibrahim's men.)

From this village a mountain shaped exactly like a pyramid can be seen standing on the horizon, sharply visible against the blood-red sunsets of the Peloponnese. It marks Pylos. Here, in 1827, the battle of Navarino takes place, and allied victory – by the French, Russian, British and Greeks – over the Turks guarantees that some sort of Greek state is established. Never again will sailing ships engage each other in such a mighty battle; it is said that great shadowy shapes, sunken ships, can still be seen on the sea floor of Navarino Bay.

The same old strands meet, plait and intertwine. War and wandering and exile, the striving for an often vague idea of Greekness, and a passionate love of that idea: Rigas Pheraios dying for it, his strangled body sinking into the Danube at Belgrade in 1798; ex-King Otto fretting for the Greece to which he was not permitted to return, wandering inconsolably, dressed in a fustanella, through his Bavarian forests. And always movement and always hardship. Peasants move to the mountains to escape the malaria and plague which haunt the valleys; later they go abroad to escape grinding poverty.

In George Drosinis's famous poem, 'The Soil of Greece', the departing migrant takes a *phylacto* as protection against all sorrow, every evil, sickness and death. The *phylacto* is a little, only a little, of the soil of Greece. But in a village near this one, a peasant about to set out for the promised land of America hurls a stone down the mountainside and swears never to return to a place which has brought him only hardship and sorrow.

Aphrodite's village. To the east a steep, stony path rises up the mountainside to one of several sparsely populated hamlets. The best time to climb this track is just before dawn, when lights stud the blackness. Soon after, a first flush of sun spreads slowly and the lights blink and disappear one by one. From darkness to light, from silence to sound: dogs bark, roosters crow, donkeys sob, small creatures (stoats, tortoises?) scuffle in the undergrowth. From the height reached after an hour's steady climbing, the village seems small, peaceful, and protected by mountains stretching away in all directions. The dawn sky, streaked with pink, marked, perhaps, by a few rosy puffs of cloud, seems almost impossibly benign. The Anglo-Saxon reader/walker is irresistibly reminded of the ending of *Wuthering Heights* and wonders how 'anyone could ever imagine unquiet slumbers for the sleepers in that quiet earth'.

The earth waking to another day under that fickle sky has, however, rarely been quiet; as for the sleepers in it, there must have been a certain restlessness. At least one murder has been committed here in recent times, although feminists everywhere would have no hesitation in calling it justifiable homicide. There have been elopements and suicides. From the caves that gape in the mountainsides guerillas would descend almost nightly on the village during the civil war.

Lower down, the olive groves are stepped in terraces along the hillsides. In summer one can walk endlessly on ochre-coloured earth, gather oregano and wildflowers, see nobody and hear nothing except the relentless shrilling of cicadas. A distant haze smudges blue mountains; here and there cypress trees stand like dark-green sentinels. The hedgerows grow high and thick, and the years have produced a tumble and twining of prickly pear, ivy, mastic and blackberry. Piles of wood, safe in the forks of trees, wait to be collected before the first rains come; sheep and donkey dung has been swept into small cones. The only sign of change is the occasional glimpse of a crumbling mud-brick house standing deserted amid the straggling remains of an orchard, a salutary reminder of the inevitability of decay.

But the name never dies. My mother-in-law is called Aphrodite Bouras. Her name has never changed: both her father and her father-in-law were called George Bouras. Her name does not appear on the family tree, where only male names are registered, but a close inspection of the edge of the fan-shaped structure reveals that she and her husband were third cousins, not sixth as she once told me. The written record clashes with her memory, with the information she was told so long ago. For she could not have examined the family tree herself: she cannot read. Nikolaos, her grandson, our second son, used to worry about this when he was a small boy. It seemed to him to be almost totally mysterious that someone so old and so wise should be unable to read. One day he went to her house and was away some time; on his return he announced sturdily, 'Yiayia *can* read – sort of. She knows all her letters. It's just that she has awful trouble joining them up into words.'

The importance of memory. And the belief in its power. We four were gardening once, George, Alexander – our third son – Yiayia and I. Alexander, then only a little boy, while scrabbling around in the dirt suddenly unearthed a fossil, a shell. He washed it and showed Yiayia the pearly ridges fused with rock. It was a pretty thing.

'You know what that means, Alexi, don't you?' asked George. Alexander looked uncertain. 'It means that once upon a time, a long, long time ago, the sea was here, probably right here where we're standing.' Alexander's eyes grew round at the thought.

'Your father's right,' added Yiayia comfortably. 'Myself, I don't remember exactly when the sea was here, but never mind.'

Yiayia used to be restless, forever on the move. There was a compulsion to fill in the day, once so crammed with activity, and then, suddenly, so empty. Two or three shopping excursions up at the *agora*, numerous visits across the road to her daughter's house, round the corner to her son's. There at least she used to sit, remembering, talking about old times, but at the end of half an hour she would be up and off, to reappear in the afternoon.

Now, increasingly, she sits in her own kitchen, or outside on the step. The pattern she once knew so well has blurred: she cannot quite follow it. Change has complicated it and now she prefers to make her own, dwelling on some details, embroidering others, bringing some features into a prominence they never had before.

One physical change she brought about herself. She took the scissors to her hair as soon as she could no longer plait it properly. She substituted one act of power and control for another: such things have always been important to her.

NOTEBOOK, WINTER 1992

Vasso has cut Yiayia's hair, or rather, finished the job already started. It is now just below collar length and strikingly attractive. I comb it for her, teasing out the knots and tangles, and say I am jealous of it, because it is so beautiful.

«Φτού! Φτού! Να μην αβασκαθή!» 'May it not be envied,' I say, for envy tempts the Evil Eye to do its worst. Yiayia's hair now sweeps back off her brow and settles in wings of pure white over her ears. Without her headscarf, she is transformed. But her family becomes coy and uneasy on the rare occasions she removes it. She herself feels uncomfortable without it and often sleeps with it on.

'Come on, Yiayia, take your scarf off,' I command. 'I want to take some photos.'

«Ελα, τώρα,» she protests, but allows herself to be persuaded. Once encouraged she is happy to sit for hours bare-headed; it is George who shifts from foot to foot and tells her to cover her hair.

In February 1992 she sits for the photographs, sometimes looking at the camera, sometimes not. It is obvious, wherever she directs her gaze, that she now is truly old. The eyes of the aged have an unfocussed quality, as though they see things, sights, spectacles that younger people cannot. Perhaps they do.

So there she sits in the most recent photos. She wears black, and her crown of white hair makes her look like an old-fashioned negative, even though the film is coloured. She has given up wearing her false teeth. She never liked them anyway, and used to wear them only in church and for visitors. Her grandchildren were always very admiring of her sleight of hand: dentures out with a quick, deft tug, enclosed in one strong hand, and slipped into a capacious apron pocket. Now skin settles on bone; nose and chin, becoming more prominent, may one day almost meet; the skin on her arms is paper-thin and powdery. She has very few reserves of strength and dressing is tiring: a button is undone, an apron string is dangling, and her thick black stockings slip into wrinkles. But in spite of her weariness she retains a strong spark of humour. For one shot she grins at the camera and lifts her eyebrows quizzically. Her expression is softer; the days of combat are over.

Older photographs, and there are only a few, show her in belligerent pose: headscarf left untied, draped over head and shoulders, fists bunched on knees, legs set apart, skirt pulled wide, shoulders set, lips compressed, eyes challenging the camera. Two or three other snapshots, cracking and wrinkling now, show her as a still-young grandmother. There were smiles for the camera then: smiles of achievement, love and pride, smiles of pleasure taken in the babies. And now Yiayia is a great-grandmother.

Last summer we took photos of Yiayia with her brother Dimitrios, the last photographs of them together, as it turned out. We went to visit Dimitrios, and Yiayia shuffled excitedly along the narrow street, for visiting is yet another activity she has largely given up. It was like a royal progress: people appeared from nowhere to kiss her hand. «Παπαδιά μας! Τι κάνετε;» The years dropped away and she returned to her role of teacher, showing me things I am, inexplicably in her view, ignorant of.

'See that?' She pointed to a round, flat stone. 'Do you know what that's for?' I shook my head. 'We used to pound our blocks of salt on that, and all the neighbourhood women used to take turns when it was time to salt the pork.' She gave a reminiscent chuckle. 'So long ago now, all that hard work.'

And then she entered the house where she had been born. It has changed but the yard has not: in the summer heat the fig tree was loaded with fruit and the pumpkin plants were spreading over the hard ground. The stone animal-houses remain unchanged, and the well, convenient hiding-place for both people and supplies in time of trouble, is still there. They sat, the old brother and sister, half embarrassed, strangely like children who had never met before, tentatively making attempts to become acquainted. The shadows deepened in the courtyard while they prodded each other's failing memories and looked back over a shared childhood.

In this place Yiayia is at the start of her particular strand of history. Here she is Aphrodite, nicknamed Bourbouni by her father. Bourbouni: little beetle. In Greece beetles are winged magic, jewels and rainbows. They flit through the air while shafts of light shoot from their luminous gold, green or rose bodies. Here, in the kitchen of the old house, is the earliest photograph of Bourbouni-Aphrodite. It is a large, framed picture, taking on a greenish tint with age: in it the priest father sits, while Aphrodite's mother, Panayota, stands behind him. The six children are ranged alongside: Vasili, Nikolaos, Joanna, Katerini, Dimitrios and Aphrodite. Aphrodite is the youngest, and stares solemnly at the camera. Her hair is cropped for school. It stands up, brushlike, around her face, emphasizing her strong, straight features, her large eyes and well-marked eyebrows – a face which will become strikingly beautiful as it develops. She is dressed in her best white smock; she wears button-up boots. Her small hand rests on her father's black-robed knee.

CHAPTER TWO
CHILDHOOD AND YOUTH

Know you what it is to be a child? . . . It is to
believe in love, to believe in loveliness, to
believe in belief . . .
Shelley, *Francis Thompson*

NOTEBOOK, SUMMER 1990

'Your job,' instructed Robyn, the geriatric nurse, 'is to allow Yiayia to replay the past, to process it.'

'Replay it!' I grumbled. 'Sometimes she's like a broken record.' And immediately felt ashamed.

'It doesn't matter. The old have that right. With luck, we'll be old ourselves one day.'

Now I think of Robyn constantly, as the replaying becomes a little muddled, as the sound falters, as the plot complicates itself and loses itself, becomes no longer linear. But the record is not the best simile. Rope is, I am sure. The threads, the strands, the knots. We are all, our young selves, not Aphrodites, but Ariadnes in possession of a ball of thread. We fix it to a lintel somehow, somewhere, and become like Theseus as we make our way into the gloom of the labyrinth, unrolling the thread as we move along.

Aphrodite's thread starts in 1908. Her identity card records that she was born in May of that year, a month suited to the name she later received, for the goddess Aphrodite was a goddess of spring. Wrapped in swaddling bands, the baby Aphrodite lay in her cradle and concentrated on the weighty matter of survival. She must have done, for other babies were born after her arrival and, sooner or later, died. She remained the youngest, little Bourbouni.

The history books say that 1908 was a memorable year. Outside Greece, various events indicated change: the Young Turk revolution took place in Turkey, and Crete, still part of the Ottoman empire, declared itself part of Greece. The old politics was no longer satisfactory. But the old economics, itself not at all satisfactory, showed little sign of changing. The same pattern prevailed: feast and famine, famine and feast, with famine always lasting longer.

Nineteen hundred and eight was a good year for currants, an important export commodity, but a very bad year for olives, wheat and tobacco. The United States and Egypt had poor seasons, too, so that the flow of money from Greek emigrants to the *patritha* slowed to a trickle. Internal Greek politics seems at this stage, at least to those not born into the tradition of cat's cradle, to become impossibly entangled.

24

In March 1913 King George I of the Hellenes was assassinated.

NOTEBOOK, 27 SEPTEMBER 1989

Yiayia has just called. She is eighty-one now and moves more slowly than before, padding about softly in black slippers. I have never seen her wear anything else but black. Today it is an appropriate costume: the whole country should be wearing it.

She stands and wrings her hands. Yesterday morning MP Pavlos Bakoyiannis, son-in-law of New Democracy Party leader Mitsotakis, was murdered, shot as he stood waiting for the lift to take him up to his office. Last night we saw television film of a stunned parliament. Mr Mitsotakis wept, red roses lay on the dead man's section of the bench, members sat silently, faces frozen in shock and grief.

'*Palia*,' says Yiayia, 'before, years ago, people were shot here, right in this village. But that was *then*. Are such things going to start all over again?'

For that dread prospect haunts the old people.

Recently the peace of a summer evening was pierced by a sharp staccato rattle. Yiayia automatically assumed it was gunfire, and closed her shutters and windows and bolted her door immediately. Later the noise was discovered to have been made by a number of spray-cans exploding. Another old woman, obsessed by tidiness as they all are, but not by concern for the environment or her own safety, had thrown the cans onto her backyard fire.

Nothing, then, is what it seems – except that final statement of death on a weekday morning in Athens. Death is death. Yet even the truth and motivation underlying this one may never be known. There is, after all, a tradition of political assassination in Greece. Capodistrias, the first president of the modern Greek state, was killed as he was entering church in Nafplion one Sunday morning in 1831. But then, assassinations had personal, as well as political, motivation. Capodistrias had tried to crush the power of the ruling Maniote family of Mavromichalis: that Sunday two of their number killed him with pistol and yataghan. Assassins and victim were well acquainted. In today's climate of terrorism this is no longer the case, and an extra dimension of meaninglessness is added to the Bakoyiannis murder.

The assassination of King George was meaningless as well. Historians view his death as a catastrophe for the young nation, for this monarch had been committed to the concept of constitutional rule and had managed to solve at least some political problems. His successor, Constantine, would not have the same skill and patience.

That large part of the Greek population which was illiterate and naturally followed its own bright ribbon of oral tradition and folklore – rather than the dull string of literacy, newspaper reports and scholarly commentaries – began to consider. They muttered and wondered about deeper meanings and patterns in life and prophecies, for folk belief held that once another Constantine sat on the throne of Hellas, the City, Constantinople, would be once more Greek.

Picture Aphrodite in 1908 and afterwards. Three times a day her mother lifted her from her cradle. Three times a day her swaddling-bands were slowly, carefully removed and rolled into a ball. It was then that the baby received her mother's full attention, was talked and sung to, and had her limbs massaged, had the modern quality time, until she was firmly wrapped in the bands again, secure and protected against the cold.

She was a baby without toys, without a pram, without bedtime stories, but one in the closest possible contact with the natural environment, playing with young goats and chickens; a baby carried everywhere and anywhere in loving arms; a baby constantly entertained, rocked and chattered to; a baby who was never alone, but was always surrounded by brothers, sisters, parents, aunts, uncles and grandparents, for all the members of the large family lived close by. As she grew, Aphrodite helped her grandmother, Asimina, who was blind, leading her, keeping her company, running errands. In Greece the young and the old are often together, for continuity is a fact of traditional life.

But Aphrodite's secure childhood did not last.

King George I died, the First and Second Balkan Wars were fought, and Greece grew and grew. She increased her territory by almost 70 per cent, as the islands of Chios, Mytilini and Samos were liberated from the Turks, and as the great cities of Thessaloniki and Yannina became Greek, as did Drama, Serres and Kavalla.

NOTEBOOK, SUMMER 1991

Vasso is away. Yiayia wants me to do her hair.

'*Can* you do it?' she asks doubtfully.

'I'll try. I used to plait my grandmother's hair sometimes,' I say, 'and she used to complain bitterly that I hurt her. Tell me if I'm hurting you when I'm combing.'

'It doesn't matter whether it hurts or not. It has to be done. Get on and do it.'

And so I do, combing carefully, then setting about the business of plaiting.

'It's still quite black underneath,' I observe.

'Fancy that,' she says. 'Well, that hair never saw the sun, I suppose. My mother, now, she was the one with the hair. As long as my arm, it was.' She extends her arm, illustrating the memory.

And now she is off, reminiscing about her mother, dead more than fifty years.

'Αχ, η κακομοίρα, ill-fated one. How she tortured herself when Vasili died. What sorrow. The neighbours told her to stop her raving and her crying, otherwise she would die, too. Well, it was only a matter of time. She really did die when she thought Dimitrios would have to go to war.'

For Aphrodite and her mother, Panayota, the only fact of any significance in relation to war and politics was that Vasili was a soldier. His history is brief and sad. Yiayia remembers herself as Aphrodite with a big brother, sixteen years older. He loved her; she used to sit on his knee. He was an embarrassed young man when his mother continued to have babies. This much Yiayia remembers. Vasili went to America at one stage but could not stay, for every night in his dreams he saw his mother dead. So he came back, obeying the signs as people then had to, but he was the one who died.

His story is marked by horror and grief. The details are not clear, but the main themes are illness, suffering and death. The First Balkan War was fought during the autumn and winter of 1912. Vasili, from Messinia, that land of long hot summers and short damp winters, endured the northern snows and a period, during the Second Balkan War, in a Bulgarian prison camp. The family does not know what other hardships he experienced or witnessed, what deeds he had to do. Soldiers often remain silent, for what is the use of trying to describe the generalities of war, the specific details of battle?

Vasili returned in 1913, apparently deeply thankful that his ordeal was over. But then he was called up again, during World War I, possibly as late as 1918, when the Greek army was in the vanguard of the allied advance on Constantinople. This time he did not go.

There are rumours of tuberculosis and blindness, but the most persistent rumour suggests that he drank tobacco juice and never recovered. It is not clear whether he intended to commit suicide, or whether he simply wanted to be too ill to serve again. The strain of striving to do greater public good than private harm had become too much. He is still loved and remembered, gentle Vasili, as a sensitive spirit with nerves too fine to endure more of war.

Much later Vasili's death-haunted American dreams came true. In 1940 Greece, against all expectations, resisted the Italian invaders valiantly. History records this, but Panayota, the bereaved mother, knew only that war had come again and that her remaining son, Dimitrios, was bound to be conscripted. Overcome by shock and despair, she suffered a fatal stroke. In ancient times, the orator Pericles tried to comfort the parents of the dead Athenian soldiers by pointing out that parents know their children are bred to varying chances. In Panayota's life, chance seems to have been mainly unvarying.

NOTEBOOK, WINTER 1992

Yiayia and I sometimes run out of things to say. When

this happens she looks at glossy magazines, carefully scrutinizing every detail, registering impressions of a lifestyle so different from her own. Recently I showed her a French decorating magazine. This time, however, she looked not at the shiny photographs but at the text, peering closely at the print.

«Αυτά τα γράμματα.» 'These letters, are different somehow,' she said.

'Well, that's French,' I replied, 'so they are different.'

'Ah. Κατάλαβα. I understand. Wait a minute, though. Look at this one! *This* is ours!' And a worn forefinger alighted triumphantly on a very large capital A at the top of the page.

On another occasion Yiayia came and started looking at Alexander's book of the Royal Melbourne Zoo, pondering the strangeness of the creatures in the photographs. She told me that her sister-in-law, Vangelena, would not even look at pictures of unfamiliar animals.

'I was looking at photos once. Lions, tigers, elephants, and Vangelena ordered me to shut the book. «Αγρια ζώα.» "Wild animals," she said. "But they're only pictures, only paper," I told her. It didn't make any difference. "We don't know the powers they may have," she said, and insisted I close the book. She didn't know anything about anything, Vangelena!'

NOTEBOOK, SPRING 1992

Today Yiayia gazes at the newsreaders on television and announces that they are her teachers, all of them.

It seems obvious to me now that old age reveals essential truths and genuine desires. Yiayia would have liked, I think, the power to enter the world of books, but has never been able to understand the state of absorption reading can produce, could never realize that interrupting reading is to drag the reader out of a dream or hypnotic trance. Or did she? She has always resented my reading and writing, for they are not *work*, and she has never had a pang of conscience about interrupting either. But then, why should she? She and I inhabit different countries with different social codes, and I am not, at this point, speaking of geography.

Now see Aphrodite on her way to school. She is privileged, spoilt, little Bourbouni, for her older sisters, Joanna and Katerini, do not go to school at all. Later Joanna uses her thumbprint when necessary. Aphrodite learns to sign her name; she learns to count to ten in French; she learns the letters of the alphabet, the capitals at least. For the rest of her life she has trouble with the little letters.

She walks up the lane, for the school is nearby, dressed in her smock, wearing her button-up boots, of which she is proud. Many children go barefoot to school, but she is a priest's daughter and appearances are important. Some mornings she carries a basket with her. In it are lumps of *pasto* – rich smoked pork – and slices of bread and cheese. This food is for the teacher, a middle-aged woman who, as far as anybody knows, receives little or no salary, and who lives, she and her ageing mother, off the goodwill of her pupils' families. She has few qualifications, very possibly none, but this does not matter.

At a later time, as a friend related the story to me, somewhere else in Greece a little girl is ordered to accompany her brother to the village school. Her job is to carry his books, for he will be a man one day and thus deserves to be waited on. Her good fortune is that he is a nervous, timid child: he begs her to stay with him. She does so, and listens and learns. By the time he becomes older and more independent, she is on her way, reading and writing and becoming addicted to the habit of both. Eventually she herself becomes a schoolteacher.

Aphrodite's father, Papayeorgi, demands, at least for a while, that his Bourbouni learn everything. But everything, for him, means the skills that will make her a good village wife. She learns to weave, embroider, knit and sew. When she is older, because she is his pride and joy, he buys her a Singer sewing machine, one of the first in the village. He pays for sewing lessons and she learns to do fine and exquisite eyelet work, cutting the intricate patterns on cloth she has woven herself, stitching and binding the edges as she bends over her treasured machine.

The struggle for schooling. A few photographs of school groups exist, and show rows of solemn-faced boys, almost invariably ragged and barefoot, but wearing smart caps adorned with a little woven owl, the bird of the goddess Athena and thus the symbol of wisdom.

'That's the peasant idea,' says George, grinning. 'Look after your head first; feet tend to look after themselves.'

'Looking after' involved, usually, at least an hour's walk up and down mountainsides, stubbing toes on rock, all in order to absorb *ta grammata* somehow.

In the first decades of the century girls were not often sent to school. Education for females was not thought necessary, and peasant ideas of honour and virtue frequently made parents reluctant to face the idea of coeducation. And here in this village are all the signs of trapped female intelligence: curiosity dwelling only on other people's lives and business, creativity finding expression in faultless housekeeping and handicrafts, desire for status satisfied in being perfect wives and mothers. After all these years of living here and talking to Yiayia, I still do not know whether she has ever had any desire for anything different. Or whether pride would prevent such an admission being made. I suspect that it has always been much easier to endure than to question.

Friends challenge me on this. 'What is the matter with such lives?' they ask. 'They're full of love and achievement: these women have accomplished what they set out to do.' And so they have. But who decided their aims? Their lives were prescribed, laid out, set down before they were born, and we will never know what has been lost, what the world has missed, because of this inability to tap potentiality, this total lack of choice.

Fifty years ago the world of mountain villages was so small that even the life of a provincial town like Kalamata, the capital of Messinia, provided evidence of miracles. One young girl, on her first visit there, was sure people were flying: she had never seen bicycles or people riding them before.

NOTEBOOK, WINTER 1990

Alexander is eight. One Sunday afternoon he and I watch the film *Cromwell* on television.

'Is this a true story?' he wants to know.

'It certainly is,' I reply somewhat ruefully.

'How do you know?'

'I learned about it at university.'

'No, you didn't.'

I would have been half flattened, I reflect, had I

contradicted my parents in such a fashion. 'What do you mean?'

'You didn't go to university.'

'Of course I did.'

'No, you didn't.'

'*Why* do you say that?' Not only is this conversation becoming ridiculous, but I am becoming exasperated.

'Because girls don't go to university.'

I gasp and almost literally fight for breath.

'*This* girl did,' I reply grimly, once capable of speech.

Yiayia thinks she stopped going to school when she was about eight. It was olive-harvest time and her parents considered her big enough to work in the groves with them. Somehow she never went back to school; there was always too much to do, and her father never helped much. He had his church work, and then there were all the people who were afraid of the Evil Eye and wanted Papayeorgi to exorcise it. People would walk down the mountainside practically every day: a baby would be restless or not eating, or somebody would be yawning incessantly, a sure sign of the Eye.

And in the mountain villages malaria epidemics were blamed on the Evil Eye. One family lost twelve children in infancy. Talismans, charms and faith were used to no avail. The children cracked like eggs, as the old people say, because of the burning fever.

'I remember,' Aphrodite told me, 'the first time they sent me to the upper village. I had to bring back some bags of olives and some branches to feed the goats with. Just me and the donkey, and I was so frightened that the donkey

34

would not know the way. But of course he did.'

'You were little then?'

'*Mikroula*! Very little. *Ti na kanoume*? What could we do? That is the way things were.'

Girls were the workers. They worked at home, in the vegetable gardens, in the olive groves, so that they could have dowries of a reasonable size. No dowry, no marriage. And marriage meant still more work.

Sociologists and anthropologists would call Yiayia a living continuum concept. Her parents, as all parents did then, worked hard to make her in the image of her mother, to give her the security of knowledge and know-how, so that when the time came she could leave them and begin her own adult, married life. It would have, this life, her parents' example and that of the holy family as a model.

NOTEBOOK, SUMMER 1987

The village is a place of little change. The seasons, rather than years, are significant. Every morning, miniature caravans, trails of donkeys, sheep and goats patter purposefully past the door, to return at twilight, the donkeys laden with hay and olive branches, sheep and goats staggering with swollen udders. The routine of Yiayia's life does not alter. She, too, goes to the olive groves. She feeds the animals and hens, she sweeps the yard, does the washing, prepares meals, makes cheese, or, turn about, makes noodles, cherry cordial, tomato paste, prepares and smokes an enormous quantity of pork. Once a year she makes soap. She crochets, gossips on the front step, naps, wakes, eats, visits the family, says her prayers and goes to bed. She coughs once, twice, three times before falling asleep.

She fasts during Lent, before Christmas, before the Beheading of St John, before the Dormition of the Virgin and before the Exaltation of the Honourable and Life-Giving Cross. Every Sunday she puts on her best black clothes, her expensive shoes, her top-quality headscarf, settles her dentures firmly in place, and walks to church. In the churchyard people kiss her hand, for she is a *papathia*; inside the church she has her own chair, near the front, for she is a *papathia*. At the appointed times during the service she crosses herself. During the Great Entrance she kneels on the mat-covered floor and makes great sweeping movements: forehead to breast, right shoulder to left.

Aphrodite's life, however, compared with the lives of some other girls and young women, was a comfortable one. Some women, not even ten years older, knew only struggle. Kyria Yannoula and her husband lived in the upper village and eked out an existence by cutting and carting firewood to Kalamata, where it was sold to the bakeries supplying the large town. The mere thought of the labour involved in that enterprise of seventy years ago is a daunting one; today the road is seven kilometres long, the mountain path not much shorter. In Kyria Yannoula and her husband's day the fuel could only be brought down to the lower village by donkey or mule, and although such animals were very willing and used to carrying enormous burdens, the return on time and labour invested was pathetically small. Selling firewood was not enough to live on: the couple also sold forked branches to a neighbouring village, where they were used to support grapevines in the plentiful and well-tended vineyards.

One day the young husband swore in disgust, said there was no future in the lives they were leading and that he would go to America in order to make some money. In 1915 he borrowed two thousand drachmae so that he could go. The marital home had been his wife's dowry and became the surety for the loan. Off he went to work in the restaurants of Chicago. This seemed the obvious thing to do, as other villagers were already working there as waiters and chefs. When he returned in 1921 he apparently saw no shame in doing the woman's work of cooking, and his wife boasted that he was the best cook in the village and that his rabbit stew had everyone licking their fingers.

Having borrowed two thousand drachmae, the young man returned with thirty thousand, very little indeed to show for six years' hard work. With that money the couple bought a grapevine and some terraces, which were not very satisfactory: the olive trees were inclined to wither and produce fruit of poor quality. But perhaps the migrant did not really care as long as he was home, for he had suffered so greatly from homesickness that when he returned to his village he immediately swapped his European-style garb for Greek traditional dress. Ever after he wore his fustanella with pride.

Kyria Yannoula's hard life continued. While her husband was away in America, she looked after their three little boys. When he came back she quickly had two more and a daughter. Later she lost two sons: one died on the Albanian front and the other in Athens during the war. 'That is why my heart is black,' she stated sadly, not long before she died at a very great age.

What did such women know of history, of the years of schism, national defeat, and the seesawing between monarchy and republic? How well did they understand the connection between the vast outside world and their own tiny, inward-looking one? It is difficult to say, but they must have known the great names: that of Prime Minister Venizelos is still referred to in hushed tones all over Greece. In the royalist Peloponnese they probably knew, at least in a vague way, of the fluctuating fortunes of the royal family. They would have known, one assumes, of the dictatorship of General Pangalos, famous, or infamous, for a brief invasion of Bulgaria and for issuing a decree that forbade women to wear skirts with hems more than a certain distance from the ground. But whatever village women knew, they knew only after it had been filtered through men's relaying of information and expression of opinion. Men were the fibres that bound the two worlds together. And did these women realize that they were never able to confront information from the outside world directly, that they could not know it in the way they knew facts in their own world?

But they must have known about Smyrna, even if they had no idea of international intrigue, knew nothing of diplomacy, of the way in which the Greek army had been only forty miles from Ankara. With supply lines stretched to the limit and unable to buy arms from Britain, even though that country had been considered a Greek ally, it had been pushed back. What the women knew, they knew because of their soldier men. Everybody had somebody in the army, for Greece was on a war footing for nearly ten years – from 1912 to 1922 – and out of a population of five and a half million, two hundred thousand men were in the army. George's Uncle Vangeli, Aphrodite's brother-in-law, was in the army then; he saw Athens and Constantinople, returned home safely, and never again travelled anywhere but to Kalamata.

Nineteen twenty-two saw the deaths of cities, of thousands of people, of a whole way of life. The Great Idea, that echo of old Byzantium and its empire, was no more; later people would remember the way in which Greeks and Turks had managed, for the greater part, to live amicably together in Anatolia and the islands nearby. Smyrna, the massacre, the desperation, the atrocities, were an example of a world gone mad. Tiny babies, their parents and grandparents all had their lives, if they had indeed escaped with their lives, irrevocably changed. An ageing man now living in Athens was, as a newborn baby, held once by his father, who was then dragged off by the Turks and never seen again. The child and his family were eventually settled in the Greek community in Romania: many years were to pass before they came to Athens.

In 1923 Greece and Turkey signed a convention which provided for an exchange of populations. Athens was almost immediately ringed by shanty towns. A million people came to Greece. It was a time of fear, doubt, bravery, anomaly. At least one historian mentions that Turkish-speaking Orthodox were forced to go to Turkey, Greek-speaking Muslims forced to come to Greece. Today, in Kalamata, the little houses built for the refugees still stand on the edges of the older part of town, and now Kalamata is home to more displaced people: Kurds, Albanians and Greek-speaking Russians from the Pondos region.

In the late 1920s there were even one or two refugees from Asia Minor in Aphrodite's village. Religion and language they had in common with the local population, but it is probable that a Peloponnesian village then seemed like a place of the harshest exile. And now old Kyrios Yeorgos from the village tells how he was put on a boat in the harbour at Smyrna. The city was burning. He had the clothes he stood up in; someone gave him a blanket.

I flip the pages of my son's final-year history textbook and struggle over extracts written in *katharevousa*; somehow I manage to get a tenuous grip on the facts, which arrange themselves into an extremely complicated series of events, featuring shifting and changing loyalties of the Western powers towards Greece. With a kind of sick fascination I absorb the difference between the 1921 rhetoric of the King of the Hellenes and the poignant folk-song sung by a grieving people after August 1922, when the Turkish offensive resulted in the rout of the Greeek army and the destruction of Smyrna.

King Constantine II, like leaders of armies everywhere, was convinced of the rightness of his cause and of the inevitability of victory. 'With the blessing of the Most High, victory will crown the struggle of the Race,' he announced. For was not the race committed to the highest ideals of freedom, democracy and justice? He stated that he was confident of divine aid, of the powers of his 'heroic army and of the invincible ethical strength of the Greek idea'.

Less than two years later the folk-songs would sing of dead youth:

> Tell my parents that I married here in Turkey,
> That I took a slab for a mother-in-law, the
> black earth for a wife,
> And two cypress trees embrace over my grave.

The mountains and fields, according to the song, were full of the bodies of young men and would never bloom again. The race would continue to struggle.

The textbook is the usual conglomeration presented to the student: photographs, documents, extracts from literature written later, first-hand accounts, attempts to explain the reasons for such horror. The explanations skim over features of the national psyche, economics and nationalism. The impression left to the casual reader is that the Greeks had been tolerated in Asia Minor, but also resented because they were so successful at business, exhibiting the same character traits as their peasantry: thrift, a determination to survive, and *poniria* – loosely defined as a type of secretiveness and capacity for cunning necessary to rural dwellers during the time of the Turkish occupation, and a great advantage when applied to business. The textbook actually states that English and French businessmen lacked this quality of *poniria* and thus were not as successful. But both Greeks and Armenians were powerless against the rise of Turkish nationalism, and against suddenly triggered mob frenzy.

The destruction of Smyrna was only the final episode. For years before 1922 poorer Greeks had been a convenient source of forced labour, or had been compelled to leave the coast and settle in the hinterland. One of the photographs shows a few mules and a long line of people trailing across what looks like a gibber plain. Later I see a documentary about the period. Jerky footage shows, among other terrible sights, a woman desperately beating a bullock which is refusing to move. Between 1915 and 1922, history records, two hundred thousand Greeks were lost.

More photographs spread across the pages. Stately buildings along Smyrna's waterfront are just visible through a pall of smoke. The pictures, of course, are black and white, and the prints are hazy – blurred with time, panic, and the limiting nature of primitive cameras. A first-hand account, however, states that the sky was blood-red from the reflection of the fire. The sea, too, would soon be tinged with red. Boats have been captured in time by the camera: two are crammed with people and one is in the process of sinking. The Turks opened fire on the people struggling in the water; one man, reaching the wharf, and trying to climb ashore, had his hands severed at the wrist by a sword-wielding Turk.

The sea was the only hope of escape, and desperate people trampled others in their attempts to get away. One woman recalled that her sister's baby, so young that it was still in swaddling-bands, was bayoneted while in its mother's arms. The young mother had no choice but to abandon the tiny corpse and continue her struggle to escape. She was able to bribe some Turkish soldiers and get the rest of her family away. Her own mother had only instruction, not consolation, to offer: 'Live, my daughter, for your other children.'

And one imagines that she did live, for that is the way mothers have to be. But even if she eventually managed to find some joy in and through her other children, I wonder how she could ever really have recovered from the horror of that moment. For it would have only been a moment. An essential part of her must have died with her murdered baby. 'There's always that thought, the wondering about what might have been,' said my aunts, both of whom lost babies because of the shortcomings of nature, rather than of man. And one added, 'I recovered because I had to, but that sense of loss will be with me, I'm sure now, until the end.'

Among the photographs of a dying Smyrna is one of the Metropolitan Chrysostom, calmly gazing at the camera as he holds a telegram from Prime Minister Venizelos in his hand. Later, when the French consul suggested that he leave in order to save himself, he refused, with equal calmness, to abandon Smyrna and his flock. 'I am here,' he said, 'in the midst of my faithful, and here I ought to stay.' He was murdered by the Turkish mob; so states the textbook. Another equally bald statement summarizes thousands of years of history: 'The day after the fire, Smyrna, as the centre of Hellenism in Asia Minor, ceased to exist.'

Old Smyrna passed into history, that history of which Marx said, 'It does nothing, it possesses no immense wealth, fights no battles. It is rather *man*, real living *man*, who does everything, who possesses and fights.' Man, in the form of King Constantine, was forced to abdicate; he was replaced by his eldest son, George. In November 1922, individual men, six politicians and commanding officers, were executed: they had risked, fought and lost.

Aphrodite grew through these years. Smyrna would have been called a *megalo kako*, a great evil. Yet this loss was an impersonal one, *makria*, far away. Far worse for the family was the loss of its own children. The eldest, Niko, had already migrated to Chicago. Dimitrios, the youngest, followed him in 1916. It was not known when they would return. As it happened, Dimitrios stayed away twenty years, returning to get married. When he arrived in America he was young enough to attend school there. Niko never came back: Aphrodite does not remember him. He married a Czech wife and had one daughter, Evelyn. Nobody knows where she is now.

And Katerini died. Aphrodite repressed her knowledge of this event, and has started talking about it only very recently. When an unmarried girl of the Orthodox faith dies, she is dressed as a bride. She lies in a white coffin under a shroud of white carnations; a wedding crown is in her hair, white candles burn at her head and feet. After the funeral sugared almonds are given to the mourners, as they are to wedding guests. Small wonder that Aphrodite, the youngest daughter, should choose, consciously or unconsciously, to forget.

She chose instead to concentrate on her elder sister's wedding. She was devoted to Joanna and spent many hours working on items for her dowry. Joanna made a good match, for her husband was the purchasing officer at the local hospital. She went to live in Kalamata, which to village girls then was a symbol of progress and luxury. Kalamata had orange groves and horse-drawn cabs. But for all that, Joanna continued her traditional life. Her husband owned land in his traditional village outside Kalamata: goats, gardens and olive groves were still a vital part of Joanna's existence.

Aphrodite's life unrolled from season to season. Little events marked stages. Her godmother, also Aphrodite, pierced her ears, inserted little sticks of oregano in them – to keep the holes open and help them heal – and issued strict instructions to keep turning the sticks. She then gave her a pair of gold earrings.

Every summer many villagers would go to the upper village, as Aphrodite would do each summer after her marriage. Her family, however, moved only a short distance away and concentrated on drying figs and picking grapes.

It seemed as if nothing would change.

NOTEBOOK, SUMMER 1991

The actor Simon Callow, while directing the film *The Ballad of the Sad Café*, says he asked the actors to 'eschew psychological complexities and to accept a world in which things happen because they do'.

The theatre critic John Peter says that for Ibsen, as for a great many European writers, the village or small town has an atmosphere of unease and claustrophobia; it is a place of thwarted ambitions, stunted lives, petty corruption and the threat of decay. American townships pre-World War II, however, are seen as decent, supportive, friendly places where simple hearts believed in simple virtues and old-fashioned values.

Out for a drive on the weekend, George and I took a break at a village *kafeneion*, somewhere between here and Kyparissia. We sat at a table behind which a grapevine spread leaves against the baking heat. There were no women present. Six men immediately engaged us in conversation, gave us directions, instructions, and refused to let us pay for our lemonade.

Further on we met a wiry old man cajoling his loaded horse along a dusty, potholed road. His face lit up at the novelty of seeing strangers. He was at pains to tell us that he had travelled: he had fought on the Albanian front in 1940. At eighty he seemed more like sixty in body and spirit, and showed the wholesome effects of hard work: with the prosperity of modern times, worry has been eliminated. Provided a man is not too greedy, is happy with his lot, he can live well. The old are reaping the benefit of their innate resistance to change: not for them the tensions and competition of ultra-modern life. A father wants his sons set up as good providers, his daughters to have good dowries; then his work is done. Ways of thinking very often remain the same, even on a superficial level, and exert an irresistible charm over the visitor.

'How far is it to the nearest village?' asks George.

'About five kilometres, I'd say. Wait a minute, though – that's five kilometres on foot, not by car!'

Each culture has its own form of dottiness. A Melbourne taxi-driver once told me that he reassured his Pommie mate by telling the worried man death was not a likely consequence of a bite from a huntsman spider.

'I put him straight. "Nah, mate," I said, "that's not on. And I'll tell yer why: that mob kicks yer to death instead!"'

At the Newcastle-upon-Tyne station I once saw a man in his sixties wearing a beret carefully angled to show off his feathered party hat. On a bus trip to Blackpool the passenger sitting behind me sang in a melodious and strong baritone for much of the way. Not one head turned, and certainly no comment was made.

In Greece, at least in villages, this dottiness often consists of approaching life at Cavafy's 'slight angle to the universe'. On Skyros, Katie, friend and philhellene, saw an elderly man bring his pet duck to the beach every day. The duck was on a lead, would have a leisurely swim in the waves, and then pet and master would go home again. While walking Ozzie the dog I met a villager who was prodding a small flock of turkeys along with a stick. We said nothing, but I imagined our trains of thought.

I: 'Why take turkeys for a walk?'

He: 'Why take a dog for a walk?'

CHAPTER THREE
LOVE AND MARRIAGE

*Marriage isn't just domesticity, or the continu-
ance of the race, or institutionalized sex, or a
form of property right. And it damned well
isn't happiness, as that word is generally used. I
think it's a way of finding your soul.*
The Lyre of Orpheus, *Robertson Davies*

NOTEBOOK, SPRING 1991

'Do you remember your wedding day?' I ask Yiayia.

The old eyes gaze into the distance, then focus on mine. Yiayia gives a half-smile.

'Yes, I can remember it, but it all seems like a dream. It's a long time ago now. How long ago is it exactly?'

'Sixty years.'

'*Oriste*! There you are. A lifetime.'

'What did you wear?'

'Ooh! I remember all that. My dress was pale pink and embroidered and my gloves were embroidered, too, but white.' She chuckles at the recollection. 'The embroidery stood out, was raised, just like the veins on my hands now.' And her forefinger lightly touches the ropelike veins on the backs of her hands. 'I had a white veil. Brides these days have given up wearing veils but I like them, don't you? My shoes were the last word in fashion: beige patent leather, *very* elegant. Oh, and I carried a beautiful bouquet of spring flowers.'

There is no photograph, but we both stand for a moment, she remembering, I imagining, trying to match description and reality.

Aphrodite was twenty-three years old when she married. Her sister and many of her friends were already married and mothers. Now it was her turn. Her life this far had followed the pattern of her mother's, with her father determining its colour, strength, security. Her father found a husband for her. She claims she knew nothing of the match until her father told her of it.

Aphrodite married Dimitrios Bouras in May 1931. Dimitrios was a mountain man; the house where he was born still stands, a solid yet graceful little mud-brick structure which seems to have been built on the edge of the world, for all that is visible from it is the great sweep of sky above and an almost equally great sweep of mountainside and valley below.

The family has a photograph of the George Bouras who built this house. There he sits in full traditional dress, nine metres of fustanella, wide-sleeved shirt, rich satin waistcoat and tasselled cap. His left hand rests on his knee, his right is tucked into his leather belt, which is a thing of beauty, skilled craftsmanship, and many sections and pockets. This costume had been purchased the hard way; he travelled to Tripolis, a distance of ninety kilometres, a journey which now takes on the gloss of epic. He walked, so the family says, and led three mules who bore six goatskins of olive oil. This was a weight of at least two hundred kilograms, worth two hundred thousand drachmae.

This George Bouras apparently died sooner than he had expected to, for at the time of his death he had not discussed the matter of the allocation of land with his two sons. Later, one of his grandsons, about to wear George's costume at a National Day celebration, found the old man's will stowed away in one of the pockets of his belt.

There is the family's link with the history of which they are so proud, for George Bouras's father fought in Tripolis against the Pasha. But it is not only history that knots, breaks, threads and unravels. Sometimes genes seem to behave in the same way. The George Bouras who died in 1948 is survived by eleven grandsons. One, his daughter's son, works his grandfather's land, uses the house, leads much the same life. It is this one, Nikos, who is truly his grandfather's grandson, for the resemblance, skipping a generation and the female sex, is startling. And while many other grandsons are scattered throughout Greece, some living in cities, Nikos is still a mountain man. At forty-eight his face is lined and his hands are thickened from forty years of work, of wresting a living from inhospitable earth. He is used to gazing long distances: fans of fine wrinkles edge his eyes. He is used to solitude: he smiles a shy smile, says little and minds his own business.

NOTEBOOK, SUMMER 1991

'Mountain people are different,' says today's George Bouras. 'People *are* different, you know.'

'How are mountain people different?' I ask.

'I've thought about this a lot. Mountain people are religious, hardworking, economical in their habits, and trustworthy. Oh, and they're modest as well.'

I grin at this last. 'You have thought about this. Why are they full of these admirable qualities?'

'They didn't have as much contact with the Turks, did they? It's obvious that they were able to exercise initiative, and control their own lives, in a way that valley dwellers weren't. And those qualities seem to have lasted.'

'What sort of characteristics do valley dwellers have, then?'

'Well, because of their situation of being in constant contact with the Turks, compromise was always necessary. They have a reputation for trickery, and for showing off. They had to be cunning and also adept at the art of making a good impression in order to survive.'

George's sisters' marriages were arranged ones. At least one prospective suitor had no chance because he came from a certain valley village.

'Did he live too far away?'

'No, he was *different*; he was a valley dweller.'

But long before then, Yiayia married a mountain man and went to live with him in a house at the very end of the lower village. At that time people ate the food they grew and produced, drew water from the well, used lamps and candles at night. Yiayia and Dimitrios shared the house with Dimitrios's parents and his brother Vangeli, and Vangeli's wife. Yiayia wove cloth for bedlinen, clothes and donkey-rugs, and began the pattern of her forty years of married life.

Now, in 1991, young George, Yiayia's second grandson, is getting married the modern way. There has been no matchmaker and no talk of dowries. But there is, of course, a pre-wedding party, and we all go.

It is hard to say what Yiayia makes of the changes, or whether she even thinks of herself and that tying of the knot sixty years ago. She did not have running water in her kitchen until 1975; now the newly-weds have a water-guzzling dishwasher, possibly the first in the village. Instead of the wooden bat Yiayia used for pounding and beating rugs and clothes, the young couple has the latest model in washing-machines. Yiayia lays one finger on each machine, but says nothing.

But in the lounge-room she pats the new furniture, blinks and then watches carefully as the drapes swish back and forth at the tug of a string. '*Ti les*! Fancy that. All these things and all of them beautiful.'

Young girls flutter about with snowy sheets and monogrammed pillowslips. Mitso, Yiayia's son-in-law, reminisces about his own wedding thirty-five years before.

'Homemade pillows,' he says ruefully, 'and nobody was very fussy about the straw stuffing. Every so often you'd be woken up by a beetle burrowing or singing directly under your head.'

A hand-crocheted filet-patterned bedspread of exquisite workmanship is spread and two little boys are promptly sat on the made bridal bed.

'What about girls?' asks the mother of a demanding only son, obviously feeling jaundiced.

'Boys are better,' retorts an elderly widow. The sour mother subsides.

Yiayia throws her share of rice and sugared almonds and deposits a 5000-drachma note on the bed. Rose petals and grains of rice settle on her black *mandili*, but she does not mind. Soon the dancing starts: she sits, claps, and taps her foot, much more uninhibited now than she was ten years ago when she was very mindful of her position and dignity. This must be one of the bonuses of old age, this letting go. Another must be the sense of achievement, witnessing the tangible result of a lifetime of work and struggle.

One hundred and sixty-four years after the Battle of Navarino the family travels to Pylos, the place by the pyramid-shaped rock, for the bride is not a villager. So far thoughts about dwellers-by-the-sea as distinct from mountain men and valley people have not been forthcoming. The church is perched high above that bay which Patrick White called the eighth wonder of the world. The bride is beautiful, the groom handsome and proud. All six of Yiayia's children are at the wedding, and seven of her grandchildren. A son and grandson are choristers; her elder great-granddaughter is a flower girl.

I wait to watch Yiayia place a white handkerchief over her black headscarf before she kisses the bride, so that the young girl will escape the curse of widowhood. But she forgets. A priest who knew Papadimitri, Yiayia's husband, chats to her after the ceremony.

'Courage, *Papathia*. You have good children, a good family.' She smiles in agreement and thanks him, but looks puzzled. Surely the time for courage is past?

She does hint, sometimes, that there is one thing left to fear.

'Sometimes I wonder, when I go to bed, whether I'm going to wake up in the morning,' she remarked recently.

'You don't have to be eighty-four to wonder that,' I replied.

Wondering that, indeed. I do not ask Yiayia whether she cares, whether she is frightened at the prospect of not waking up. I have already started not to care, have started longing for oblivion and getting insomnia instead, but I do not wish to discuss such matters with her: she will think me a discontented, neurotic fool.

History registered, recorded and now remembers the Great Depression. Greece's economy, never robust, suffered once again. There was a reduced demand for all the chief exports – currants, tobacco and olive oil – and a decrease in receipts from shipping, and from emigrant remittances. The United States had imposed quotas on migration. Thus two lifelines, to which peasant families had been clinging for years, were severed.

The political scene was as complicated as ever. Venizelos achieved some agreement with Greece's neighbours, survived an assassination attempt, but died in exile in Paris in 1936. The monarchy was restored in December 1935. General John Metaxas became prime minister. The strained political atmosphere of the time was not helped by the deaths of several senior politicians. Against a backdrop of labour unrest and stalemate in Athens, where both the populist and liberal parties had held secret talks with the communists, the latter called a 24-hour general strike as a protest against proposed legislation to introduce compulsory arbitration in labour disputes. On 4 August 1936, a day before the proposed strike was to take place, Metaxas, with the consent of King George II, suspended key articles in the constitution, imposed censorship, and dissolved parliament. Parliament did not sit again until 1946.

Metaxas's vision was one of a third Hellenic civilization which would combine the virtues of both Ancient Greece and Byzantium. It was his ambition to impose Germanic-style discipline and efficiency on Greek character and society, which he saw as being extremely individualistic and lacking in any sense of corporate loyalty. He enjoyed being known as Leader and National Father, and in 1937 had himself proclaimed First Peasant and First Worker.

Membership of the EON (National Organization of Youth) was compulsory for those between the ages of eight and twenty, and the official line of the Metaxas regime was one of hostility towards liberalism, communism and party government. It was a familiar pattern, made even more familiar by the burning of books which took place in 1936. The usual volumes were consigned to the bonfires: those by Marx, Freud, Shaw, Gorky, Dostoevsky, Tolstoy and Darwin.

During this same period, family history registered and now remembers the facts of struggle and survival in Chicago. Those years stayed with Yiayia's brother Dimitrios forever.

'Some of the sights I've seen,' he would say, shaking his white head. 'How *o kosmos* suffered. How mothers and fathers did anything, and I mean anything, to get food for their children. Well, it's natural, isn't it? Who can bear to see a child starve?' And he would shudder at the recollection. 'I was lucky. Being a waiter, I always managed to get something to eat, even when the breadlines were stretching for blocks.'

The other brother, Nikoloas, did not return. He and his Czech wife can be seen as victims of history who would never see their homes again. And now all we know is that Niko took to reading and philosophizing in later life, and spent his retirement either in libraries or deep in conversation with his friends. Occasionally I think of the Czech wife and mother trying, and failing probably, to get to know the Greek housewives of the Chicago of the twenties and thirties, for an American octogenarian also married to a Greek from this village maintains that they were extremely conscious of their Greekness, and guarded it, their secrets and their recipes fiercely.

In Aphrodite's village during the thirties, nothing happened and everything happened. By the end of the decade the house at the end of the village was home to six children, three for each couple. These births were apparently straightforward: the mothers went into labour, the midwife came and the babies were born. Then Aphrodite and Vangelena enjoyed the only pampering they would ever get: for forty days after a birth the mother looked after her baby, while everybody else looked after her.

And at some stage during the late thirties Aphrodite and Dimitrios moved to the house where she still lives. It was bought for them by their fathers, the other house apparently having become too small to accommodate growing families. Today's George Bouras, his parents' fourth child, was born in this 'new' house. Built in 1878, it used to be a shop and is right on the street: now Yiayia gazes out of the window, looking at a scene that is both familiar and strange.

NOTEBOOK, SPRING 1992

There are some questions that can never be asked. I have not asked them of my mother, as she did not ask them of hers. Still less could I ask them of Yiayia. And for some questions, answers travel only part of the distance.

Years ago, I asked, 'What did your husband call you?' For I had never heard her first name used.

'What do you mean?' The customary note of irritation I chose to ignore.

'Did he use your first name at all?'

'Of course not. He called me *Papathia*.'

'What did you call him?'

'Papadimitri, of course. What else should I have called him?'

The note of irritation had risen to one of challenge. I made no reply. There seemed none to make. But inwardly I cried, 'Always? Did you *always* call each other by these formal social labels? Did your public personae accompany you to bed?'

Yiayia often reads my mind. She looked at me, daring me to open my mouth. I quailed and dropped my gaze. Some questions can never be answered.

Now that I reread these notes it seems obvious, although it has taken me years to digest the fact, that communication in an oral, traditional society is startlingly direct. There is no distance between people and distance cannot be achieved. The bolt-hole of a letter (I'll write rather than phone) vanishes. As well, there is very little distance between the public and the private. In a traditional society you are your role and social position: a priest's wife, in Aphrodite's case. In modern capitalist society you are your work, you are the sum of your achievements. Yiayia is her status, I am my power, and we each think what the other has is inadequate.

NOTEBOOK, SUMMER 1991

Katie said, 'Was the marriage a happy one?' Here is
one question that can be asked of an observer but so
far never has been. And how to answer?

'I don't know,' I replied carefully. 'What does the
word happy actually mean when applied to that sort
of marriage? I imagine that the notion of romance was
unheard of, or at least meaningless, and just as well.'
Levels of propriety in three-generation households,
where the husband's unmarried brothers were likely to
be living, meant that there were never any overt dem-
onstrations of affection made between husband and wife.

I asked George. He said it was a happy marriage.
Well, he would, wouldn't he?

'Did they ever fight?'

'They argued,' he said.

'Who won?'

'She did. She was the boss. But my father didn't
seem to mind.'

I begin to meditate moodily on the subject of boring
old Byron. Surely Lady Caroline Lamb was overstating
the case when she said he was mad, bad and dangerous
to know, but this notion of love being woman's whole
existence has been damaging, I concede. Molière, I
have just read, considered that the great ambition of
women is to inspire love. Where did they get off, these
two? Never mind: Yiayia wouldn't have given a fig for
either of them. If she could read, she would surely
agree with the following description of medieval
society in England, written by Brian Stone:

*Where life is lived on a subsistence level, man has no
motive for elevating to a pedestal one who fulfils the*

*necessity of his bed, board and field labour, however
close his soul to hers. It was a poor Paris minstrel who
said, 'Love is only for the rich.'*

'Look,' says a village friend, 'then men only wanted
women for the bedroom, the kitchen and the fields.
There wasn't anything else.'

One of my neighbours has been complaining about her niece.

'She is *so* difficult. She doesn't want to marry any of
the nice young men her father brings home for her. Not
one.'

My sister-in-law is also complaining: her son is not
married. She lists his numerous attributes and assets
regularly. Her talk is of dowries, numbers of flats, blocks
of land.

«Ο έρωτας δεν παίζει ρόλο;» I asked. 'What about love?'

'How can anyone fall in love here?' she said. 'Gossip,
a very small circle, a closed environment, δεν γίνεται, it's
not on.'

'Still,' I commented, 'in the 1990s, to marry like that.
It all seems so much like shopping.'

«Τι νά κανουμε;» she queried airily, making, as Greeks
so often do, her answer a question. 'What can we do?'

Kyria Ariadne is a year older than Yiayia. She is small and
wiry with snapping eyes and a wide streak of independence.
She is still, as the Greeks say, as frisky as a lamb. Not for
her the black headscarf decreed by village society; in winter
she wears a knitted cap and in summer she goes bare-headed.
She sits and talks, smiling and sighing over her memories.

'People can say what they like about stepmothers. I can hardly remember my natural mother. She died, the ill-fated one, when I was just seven. My little brother was not even two, and I *can* remember the struggle I had trying to feed him with a bottle arrangement. He didn't like it, poor little thing. But about stepmothers. My father married again and he couldn't have chosen a better woman. A golden woman, she was, may God forgive her her sins. She had children of her own, but loved us all equally. And I never went along with this half-brother, half-sister nonsense. We were all brothers and sisters together.'

In her youth Kyria Ariadne was well-off, at least by village standards. Her father was a businessman who also owned a taverna and two hundred acres of land. The whole family worked in the taverna, and at harvesting grapes and drying currants. In 1931 Kyria Ariadne's dowry was 120,000 drachmae, enough to buy two houses.

Although her marriage was arranged, Kyria Ariadne's father seems to have been rather advanced in his views. It is obvious that he needed her labour, but this fact also meant that she was mixing in village society in a way that not every father, and certainly not Aphrodite's, would have thought desirable.

Kyria Ariadne was interested in fashion, music, dancing and having a good time. She smiles widely and chuckles, delighted by her memories.

'I can remember all my dresses, *paithaki mou. Ach*, what beautiful ones I had, and I made them myself. One, you just *should* have seen it, *agapi mou*. A perfect blue it was, with ever such a pretty train at the back. Just brushed the heels of my shoes it did, and of course the hemline was shorter at the front. The first Sunday I wore it to church all the men were struck dumb, poor things. You must come up and see my photos.'

And on the wall of a bare room that contains a narrow bed and little else, a large photograph hangs. There she is, the Kyria Ariadne of sixty years ago, posing carefully for the camera, as is her mustachioed fiancé. The photographer's artist has tinted her clear complexion with a subtle glow; fine bones, straight brows and large eyes are framed by a beaded cloche; her dress, another source of pride, is a rich coral. At that time, she was still playing her mandolin and learning the latest dances from a school in Kalamata. 'Oh yes, I learned them all, the fox, the fox-anglais, the charleston.' This was an unusual girlhood and womanhood, to say the least, and must have seemed, to girls like Aphrodite, almost dangerously sophisticated. No photographs were taken of Aphrodite's engagement or wedding.

The privileged life did not last. Kyria Ariadne, who had been loved, petted and pampered, was cordially loathed by her mother-in-law. Mothers-in-law who have struggled and suffered through lives of hardship resent what they see as spoiled daughters-in-law, and the pattern of establishing authority over a young girl repeats itself: after all, the mother-in-law herself has been through it, has been at the beck and call of her own mother-in-law. That is the way things were.

'She hated me,' says Kyria Ariadne soberly, 'and she was deceitful. She'd make me presents of shoes – with nails in them. And she was determined, absolutely determined, to make a shepherdess or cowherd out of me.' She gives a short, grim laugh. 'I could write a book, I tell you.'

This must have been something else that her *pethera* resented. Kyria Ariadne was permitted only a few years' schooling at the local primary school, but she never let those hard-won skills go. Instead she built on them. She has written letters all her life, writing from Greece to her daughter in Australia, writing from Australia, during a long stay there, to her son in Greece. She reads voraciously, and is presently engrossed, she tells me, in a long, involved story set in the fourth century BC. She is a far greater reader than either her daughter or granddaughter, both of whom are much more educated than she.

NOTEBOOK, SPRING 1991

Yiayia was never a shepherdess, although many women were, and some of the older ones still are, taking turns with their husbands in the care of sizeable flocks. One of these is a relative of Yiayia's, Kyria Roula.

At lambing time I often meet her toiling up and down between her house and the shepherd's hut and fold, which are tucked away into the rocky hillside. Perhaps she is fifty, perhaps not. Her hair is scraped back under a drab headscarf. Her face is weathered and tanned, white lines fan around her eyes, her figure has been stretched shapeless by childbearing, and two of her teeth are missing.

Yet hers is a contented spirit, and her face falls in soft lines, not hard ones. She chats and laughs, glad of some company: a hundred sheep provide little entertainment, although I was once mightily diverted by the spectacle of two of the rams fighting. Supported by ewes on either side, at back and at front, they would fall back and then attack, rearing up with their horns crashing, almost clanging and then locking. Kyria Roula's husband, Panayioti, usually a dour, silent man, broke into a full-throated bellow, and shied, not just stones and pebbles, but full-sized rocks at the recalcitrant males. But Kyria Roula has *isychia*, quietness and tranquillity, what every Greek woman wants.

They want *isychia* at home, they want *isychia* in politics.

So do some men. Thanassi, another shepherd, is one of them. He made a brief attempt to live in Athens, but gave up the effort very quickly in horror and disgust. Ozzie the dog and I meet Thanassi regularly on our wanderings. Once we crept past him as he lay spread-eagled, fast asleep, in the shade of a tree.

Thin and wiry as a whippet, Thanassi walks and runs jerkily, always with knees bent. He is like many a mountain man: very fine-boned, flesh hardened into muscle and sinew, eyes lost in wrinkles and creases. Focussing and counting does that. He can often be seen in the main street, carefully carrying two kerosene tins brim-full of sheep's milk to a cheese-making housewife. In rainy weather he gets about with his black umbrella on his back, the handle wedged between his scrawny neck and frayed coat-collar. Summer and winter he wears a commando-style camouflage baseball cap.

Thanassi usually signals me without a word. I retreat or advance according to his directions, like one of the flock myself. The sheep, black and murky-cream in colour, like so many perambulating Flokati rugs that have yet to be combed or washed, huddle together very obediently as I pass. Thanassi did say '*Efharisto poli*' once and his face nearly cracked with the effort.

Australian farmers have been amazed at the sight of such well-trained sheep.

'Look at them,' said Barry, my farmer uncle, on a visit to the village. He scratched his head. 'Perhaps these flamin' animals are not as dumb as we think, eh? Or could it be that Greek sheep are more intelligent? Nup, we can't have that!' And he gazed raptly as Thanassi turned his back and walked away. The sheep all ran after him, as if protesting the withdrawal of love.

Yiayia kept goats nearly all her life, having sold her last one only three years ago. She always became deeply attached to her goats, cossetting them as if they were babies. And they are indeed lovely animals, with their curious, calm gaze, their flightiness, their mercurial tempers and their daintiness. For sixty years care of the goats took up a large part of Yiayia's day, and even now village women form a steady supply-line carrying hay, olive branches and vine-leaves, or tempting morsels like orange-peel and water-melon to these mainstays of the rural round.

NOTEBOOK, SUMMER 1980

The billy-goat who has a harem close to Yiayia's house is a satanically ugly beast who seems to survey the fif-teen to twenty nannies tethered in his olive grove with an air of cool disdain. Such vanity is not always war-ranted, it seems. Yiayia's nanny has come back from her sojourn, but is now bleating incessantly.

'What's the matter with her?'

'Tch!' She gives her characteristic noise of impatience. 'What a nuisance! She hasn't conceived. Now I'll have to take her back.'

NOTEBOOK, WINTER 1981

The nanny's date of confinement is drawing near and it is hard to tell who is more restless, goat or owner. Yiayia creeps downstairs by torchlight two or three times each freezing night to see if labour has begun.

Today Yiayia tells me to watch the goat carefully and to let her know if the onset of labour seems imminent.

'Um, how will I know?'

Once again, an impatient click of the tongue. 'She'll start pawing and stamping the ground, naturally.'

In due course this happens. I ask if I may watch. Yiayia huffs and puffs slightly at this unusual request, but tells me to hide myself behind the double doors leading into the cellar. She keeps up a constant flow of encouragement and commiseration.

'You poor old thing. Come on now. Keep trying. Ach! Ill-fated one. It hurts, doesn't it?' This goes on for some time while the goat struggles and bleats.

Squatting behind the battered doors, I suddenly see Yiayia shrug her shoulders resignedly and roll up one black sleeve. Her right hand disappears in one quick movement and then reappears almost as quickly, gripping the head of a steaming, wet bundle.

'Tch. Enormous. No wonder you needed help, my poor girl. Try again now. I'm sure there's another one in there.'

And there is. A tiny weakling slithers out and plops helplessly onto the cold stone. The first-born is staggering erratically but purposefully towards its mother, but the second is gasping feebly and seems about to give up its very short struggle for life. Yiayia picks it up tenderly, wraps it in a bit of sacking and carries it into the warmth of the kitchen, where it takes up residence beside the hearth. It has a drink of milk; its mother partakes of camomile tea.

Ten years later, in 1991, when Yiayia was beginning to fail a little, I offered to take the current nanny to the billy. Yiayia consented reluctantly, the goat herself not at all. I sweated and strained at the tether; the air was thick with the great Australian adjective as I tried to make the beast budge. Eventually we formed a strange procession: I pulling, Alexander pushing, and Yiayia laughing with great satisfaction at our incompetence.

I also offered to feed the goat night and morning, but Yiayia could not bear this usurpation of her power.

'You can't, you don't know anything about all this,' she said complacently, and did the work herself.

NOTEBOOK, AUTUMN 1985

The donkey is in trouble. I am alarmed to see Yiayia doctoring him with large doses of Coca-Cola and the garden hose at the relevant ends of his alimentary canal. The donkey loves the Coke, but has more than a few reservations about the hose.

'This beast,' states Yiayia grimly, 'is going to die, curse him, and how we will ever get his corpse out of this cellar, I do not know.'

George is duly summoned and ordered to take the donkey to a piece of land some distance away and tether him to an olive tree. George obeys.

Later, the weather is dreadful. Storms, lightning, thunder, copious rain. The donkey must be dead; how could he possibly survive all this? Eventually the rain stops. George goes tremblingly to the olive grove, fearing the worst, but finds the donkey in rude health, happily standing hock-deep in ordure, braying a welcome.

Such incidents involving animals, the care of them, the daily routine, were part of Yiayia's life for over sixty years. For a very long time she remembered them, telling them, retelling them, embroidering, adding, subtracting. Now that memory, that precious storehouse of the oral/illiterate person, is failing; it is still the routine which is followed and recalled. Births, deaths, people and events are more often than not confused, but the habit of work never is. Nor are the habits of leisure: the church and gossip. The church, I was to discover, was essential because its rites accompanied life's most important events. Dogma counted for little; gossip, I was also to discover, counted for a great deal, and was almost as important as religion.

Yiayia fainted in church once, sliding gently from her chair onto the floor. Whether the heat of summer or her high blood pressure was to blame, nobody could decide. She herself was not concerned about the fact that she had fainted, but she trembled at the thought of what might have happened as a result of the fall.

'I might have hurt myself badly. I might have broken my head!'

The more she thought about it, the greater the likelihood of it happening seemed, the more miraculous her escape. 'It's a wonder I didn't do myself some damage!'

'No wonder about it at all,' retorted her cousin, Kyria Alexandra, widowed, slightly younger but with indomitable spirit. She is quite lame, but walks the village streets slowly and determinedly, leaning on a worn walking-stick. 'You know as well as I do that our Orthodoxy protects us from all harm, from every evil.' «Η θρησκεία μας είναι ζωντανή».

'Once I was walking down the street in Kalamata,' Kyria Ariadne volunteered, 'just going about my business, when suddenly I couldn't move. I was completely frozen, and there, right in front of me was the Panagia, our Lady, wearing a headscarf. At that time my daughter, my only daughter, had just left to get married in Australia. I was in a dreadful state. But I stood there in the street and our Panagia comforted me. She told me that I would have three years of suffering and worry, and that was true, I did. But she also told me that my daughter would have the sort of life I could not even dream about, and that turned out to be true, too. My daughter's life has been very happy and comfortable. She's worked hard but she's had great rewards, while we here had to work hard always and our only reward was survival.

'Anyway, some time later I was lighting a candle in the Church of the Archangels, and then, just as suddenly as I had seen my vision, I caught sight of an icon of the Panagia exactly as I had seen her in the street, headscarf and all. I had been in that church and never seen that icon before, mind you. I was ready to collapse from the shock; other women in the church were holding me up and waving smelling-salts under my nose. But this was my human weakness. After all, it was only one more proof of what every Orthodox knows to be true: our religion is a living one.' «Η θρηεκεία μας είναι ζωντανή.»

Aphrodite's village, like most others, has a main church and is ringed by smaller ones. The main one is dedicated to the Saints Theodore, while the outer limits of settlement are marked by chapels dedicated to St Nikolaos, St John, St Dimitrios, St George and St Konstantine. The convent of the Prophet Elijah crowns the highest point; it has its own chapel of St Nektarios, but these days a complement of only three nuns. Once convent life was seen as an escape route for those girls who did not wish to marry, or, more often, for those who could not marry because of poverty or disability. Nuns elsewhere practise handicrafts: in the Kalamata convent they weave silk and linen in cool, high-ceilinged rooms. Tourists come to gaze and chat; the scent of orange blossom drifts gently, and bees busy themselves in the garden. Here, however, the nuns are village women leading patterned traditional lives: one shuttles back and forth on her donkey between the convent building and its piece of land.

The chapels are used once a year, on the relevant feast day, when bevies of village women descend on them to do a thorough cleaning and deck doors and icons with as many flowers as can be found. Aghios Georgios is Yiayia's favourite chapel, George being the name of her father, father-in-law, son, nephew and grandson. It is also a very pretty place; whitewashed and plain, it sits on a hill. Sloping away from it are olive trees that flash and turn, silver and green, on all but the stillest of days. On the flat land grapevines march in rows, and ploughing and culti-vation form an expanse of patchwork. The scene might almost be part of a painting or a piece of embroidery: one gum tree and clumps of gorse are in the foreground; cypresses stand on either side. A path leads down to the fields.

It seems likely that this chapel of St George is the same one mentioned in a popular story. It used to be the custom that women took their sick children to the chapel of St George on the feast day of 23 April and rolled them down the hill, after which the children were miraculously restored to health. One woman, fearful of injury to her child, rolled a large pumpkin down first. Nothing happened to the pumpkin, so, relieved and reassured, she sent the child in its wake. But the child died of its injuries, the mother's punishment for being of such little faith.

NOTEBOOK, SUMMER 1981

Yiayia gossips. Everybody gossips. I, too, am a gossip but feel left out, for my gossip is about trivia. Gossip here is not, as today's sessions prove. Nineteen-year-old Persephone has dared to find herself a husband without consulting father, mother or matchmaker. Her father beats her, then beats his wife because this shocking development is largely his wife's fault: she has been irresponsible, has failed to exercise sufficient vigilance.

Yiayia gets all the details from a relative who seems to be the village equivalent of AAP or Reuters. I feel that the whole village hearing about this episode must be very upsetting for the girl. I become irritable.

'Why does Epaminondas have to gossip so?' I ask. 'I don't see or understand the necessity for it.'

Yiayia bends a pitying look on me and snorts slightly at this evidence of my obtuseness.

'Well, if he didn't talk about such things, how would *I* get to know about them?'

That need to know. That sense that the word is powerful, with the ability to create, to dramatize, to draw up the threads of a person's particular history and tie them into a knot that will be remembered later, no matter how long the unravelling process may take. In this society it is the externals that are important: you are what people say. Gossip enhances life, makes people larger than life, adds to the overall tapestry of history. Gossip is delight in the story; words are actual occurrences and events, not symbols seen on the blackboard of the literate person's mind. And what other people think of you is a more accurate guide than any attempt at self-analysis. What kind of person are you? Ask other people: they are more qualified to say. Judgement comes from without, not from within.

NOTEBOOK, SPRING 1991

We are all worried because Yiayia is ill. She is suffering from vertigo and high blood pressure. We go back and forth to the house, supervising and checking.

Today's scene: I check the yard and kitchen, call her name, go upstairs to find her. She is not there. I am puzzled, and the beginnings of worry start to niggle at me. I call again, and finally throw a quick glance over the wall of the yard into the animals' quarters. My horrified gaze lights on her, face-down, fully conscious, but quite unable to get up. I squeak in alarm and rush to her. She is not at all pleased to see me.

'Be quiet,' she hisses.

'Whatever for? Why ever didn't you call out? You *must* have heard me!'

'Sst. *Sou leo*. Be quiet, I tell you. People will hear. And I don't want them to. They'll say I'm drunk.'

'You? You're a *papathia*, a very respectable old woman. What *are* you talking about?'

She eyes me balefully. 'You've been here so long and you still don't know a thing. This is a village, and everybody here talks about everything and everybody else. Now get me up.'

It is what is said that is important. It has its own truth, which lies in its effects rather than in its strict accuracy.

Christa Wolf wrote, 'What is past is not dead; it is not even past.' But past and present merge and melt into one another in strange ways. In the village there are fifteen old-style *kafeneia*, some scarcely more than a doorway in a stone wall; there is also a lilac-painted, curtain-bedecked, wrought-iron-and-plastic-decorated pizzeria. Donkeys still bear their burdens of wood, hay and olive branches along the narrow streets, but now there are fewer of them and they have to be cajoled and manoeuvred past the trucks and vans which ply back and forth, delivering goods to shops that once provided only the most basic of necessities. When the saddler, who also shoes the local horses, is no longer able to work, there will be no one to take his place. The number of cars has quadrupled in the last ten years, and now young women drive them. The ploughman has retired; a young man and a small tractor have replaced him.

The blacksmiths, the cooper and the cabinet-maker have all gone. Now nobody requires a horse-drawn freight service, but the family whose members drive the freight van between Athens and the village are descended from hard-working men who steered their horses and carts along unsealed roads to Kalamata with monotonous regularity. The tinkers, too, have disappeared, so now there is no one to polish copper or supply the utensils that were once a village girl's pride and joy.

The gypsy women still come, looking rainbow-prosperous in voluminous, billowing skirts, wearing hooped earrings and flashing smiles, selling baskets and begging a little olive oil here, an egg or two there. The gypsy men still come to mend chairs, but once upon a time they used to make them. These days it is more profitable to sell carpets and plastic chair-and-table sets from the back of a van, for village girls now prefer to learn to type or operate a computer, than to weave or do raffia work. The fishmonger still comes twice a week, but now a taped message blares from the microphone fixed to the front of his utility truck. 'Fish, Kalamata fish.'

In Yiayia's youth the village shops were more like the Kalamata market as it still is. The general store, the *pantopoleion*, was an Aladdin's cave of sacks and boxes spilling over with rice, sugar, macaroni, bran, pollard, corn, chick-peas, kippers, salt-cod, sardines, lentils of all sorts and sizes. Now the Kalamata market has speckled eggs in wire baskets, and plastic bags of water tied to the legs of trestle tables so that mounds of fruit and rows of vegetables can be sprinkled regularly. Fowls lie, feathered heaps of resignation, their feet secured with string; they will be borne off, heads dangling, to their fate. Old yiayathes sit on boxes and sell seedlings: flowers, herbs, vegetables. One is always there selling sprigs of fuchsia and miniature succulents in rusting powdered-milk containers: each plant comes with a liberal sprinkling of sheep manure.

Some things change, some remain the same. In certain market shops it is still possible to buy a little heap of powdery dye. The shopkeeper places a square of newspaper carefully on the scales, and measures out the required quantity and colour, then twists the paper expertly at both ends. Shops on either side might be selling colour television sets, or Benetton clothes packaged in designer plastic. More and more roads are penetrating mountain fastnesses, so that people who live along the shores of Messinian Bay reach Kalamata in forty minutes instead of taking four or five hours by donkey or boat. Now they come to shop, instead of visiting only in dire emergencies to see a doctor or dentist.

But taxi-drivers refuse to wear safety belts; instead they cross themselves when passing a church.

NOTEBOOK, SUMMER 1989

Knowledge of a certain sort is not past. We arrived
back from Constantinople yesterday. I brought Yiayia
a bottle of holy water from a Greek church. Near this
church a shepherd had been grazing his flocks and
washing himself in a stream of muddy water. The
earth was hard and clay-coloured, just as it is here.
Outside the church walls sat two Greek-speaking beg-
gars. Today I tell Yiayia all this, and how we attended
Divine Liturgy at the Patriarchate: one man had burst
into tears after meeting His Holiness Dimitrios I.

'But this water came from the Church of the . . . of
the . . .'

'Of the Life-Giving Spring,' finishes Yiayia, and
tells me the story we, the tourists, had been told of the
monk who had been frying fish when the city fell. At
this climactic moment the fish leapt from the frying-
pan into the deep waters fed by the spring, where their
descendants may still be seen today.

'I didn't know you knew all that,' I say sheepishly.

'Well, I've been taught it, haven't I? I've heard it,
and I've learned it and remembered it.'

Now see Aphrodite, the young mother of four, working
constantly: baking bread, tending animals, going to the
olive groves, looking after the children, fetching water from
the well, washing and weaving, always weaving: blankets,
sheets, saddle rugs, mats and carpets. She is in a constant
mist of fatigue, but does not expect anything else. It takes
about twelve hours to thread looms and even then the
weaving is not always easy. As in weaving, so in life. There

is a Greek saying for life's difficult stages: the knot came to the comb. 'Ηρθε ο κόμπος στο χτένι.

NOTEBOOK, SUMMER 1991

'Somebody said that people who are in love should never marry,' muses Katie.

'I thought you said that,' I comment.

'Oh, I did and still do. Arranged marriages are the thing. And when couples whose marriages have been arranged fall in love, well, that must be sheer bliss.'

'Surely, speaking from a position of pure logic, they should then divorce?'

'Get away, you!'

Then see Aphrodite later, much later. It is 1972 and she is dressed in her best, ready to visit her husband, who is in hospital. Pericles, her eldest son, has to tell her, somehow, that Papadimitri has died during the night. '*Oxi!*' she screams aloud in protest and shock. She hurls her handbag away from her, way out into the street, a woman's feeble gesture against Fate and the Furies. She never wears colours again. And every morning she ties her widow's black *mandili* under her chin and faces the day alone.

CHAPTER FOUR
WAR AND FAMILY

The simple stupidity and innocent amenability
of ordinary human nature lends itself to being
perverted . . . If you are gullible and not
very good at saying no you can lose your
identity and get turned into a killer punchdrunk
with efficiency.
Sunday Times, *John Peter*

The facts are these: Metaxas tried to remain neutral when war broke out in 1939. He was, after all, pro-German. He also did his best to ignore a series of Italian provocations, one of which was the torpedo attack on the Greek cruiser *Elli* while she was anchored off the island of Tinos in August 1940. But he could not ignore the ultimatum delivered by the Italian minister at three a.m. on 28 October 1940, and his firm '*Oxi!*' became the nation's battle-cry.

It is also a fact that the Greeks defeated the Italians and

that a reluctant Hitler had to come to the rescue of the latter.

Mussolini had miscalculated: his intelligence reports had indicated that the Greek army was both low in morale and poorly equipped. He had not reckoned on the efficiency of General Papagos, or on the wave of patriotism that swept the Greek nation. It is difficult to think of a time when Greece was more united than in the winter of 1940–41.

It is recorded that in January 1941 Churchill offered Metaxas the aid of British troops. Metaxas declined the offer because he did not wish to provoke Hitler, but by the end of the month Metaxas was dead and history developed very differently as a result.

The dates:

6 APRIL	Hitler's troops invade Greece in Operation Marita.
18 APRIL	Prime Minister Koryzis commits suicide.
27 APRIL	The German army enters Athens. Writer Penelope Delta commits suicide.
20 MAY	The German airborne attack on Crete, Operation Mercury, takes place.
31 MAY	The swastika is torn down from its flagpole on the Acropolis.

By the beginning of June 1941 all of Greece was in German, Italian and Bulgarian hands.

NOTEBOOK, WINTER 1992

I have been reading Niko's history textbook again. Without the women there would have been no victory. All Greek women should become like the women of the Pindos, wrote one admiring journalist. A diarist noted that one of the women carrying ammunition where transports could not go was eighty-eight years old. He also noted the typical communal family effort: one yiayia minded two little children while their mother made bread for the army by the light of two candles in a glass. Mothers who were not near the war zone farewelled their sons and did not shed a tear.

'Sparta lives again,' reported the *Free Tribune* newspaper. 'Mothers show their sons the path of duty and simply wish them *Kali niki*. Good victory.'

When the Germans entered Kalamata and began to fan out through the surrounding countryside and valleys, the villagers fled to their ancestral homes in the mountains, conforming to that age-old pattern of advance and retreat, movement forth and back, and, if fortune smiled, forth again. Fifty years later a Greek businessman, resident in this village but widely travelled in the Middle East, expressed his sympathy for the Kuwaitis at the time of the Iraqui invasion. 'All that sand and flatness,' he said, sadly. 'They've got nowhere to go, nowhere to hide.'

Picture Aphrodite then, readying her young family, nine-year-old Vasso, eight-year-old Pericles, four-year-old Aspasia, three-year-old George, and baby Niko. Picture Papadimitri organizing the animals and loading them, trying vainly to estimate how much food they should take, to think of what they would need for an indefinite stay in that small stone house perched on the edge of the world where no one had lived for some time, his parents having moved down to the house in the valley. Rain falls, the path is steep and slippery, children and newborn goats have to be helped or carried.

Aphrodite and her family, together with her brother-in-law and his family, stayed in the little stone house on the mountainside for a month. While they were there, the retreating allied forces were trying to defend Kalamata. Along the waterfront, where today fleets of motorbikes roar past hundreds of coffee drinkers, the battle raged for quite some time. Eventually, however, the allies were defeated, and the hills and olive groves around Kalamata became hiding places for soldiers desperately hoping and waiting for boats to take them to Crete. Many, however, were captured and trucked to German and Austrian prison camps.

Stan McDonald was one of the soldiers captured just outside Kalamata. In a letter he recalls being marched through the main street together with other Australian, New Zealand and British soldiers. And he also remembers the women of Kalamata being more demonstrative than the men on that occasion. 'They clapped and cheered us and threw us little bits of food, and we all knew that they had precious little for themselves. The Germans were pushing and shoving them with their rifle-butts, but they didn't care. I've been reading Nicholas Gage's *Eleni*. What a brave, selfless woman . . . The women of Kalamata were all Elenis to me.'

The action of the women was another gesture against Fate, in defiance of what often seemed to be the inexorable processes of history. The swaddling-bands of infancy can be seen as a symbol of such women's lives: at climactic moments they are able to throw them off.

'I hate history, because it makes man feel helpless in the stranglehold of hatred,' wrote Anaïs Nin. At the outbreak of war she cleaned her typewriter, with the intention of going on loving and writing until the bombs fell. She was not, she said, going to quit or abdicate, or play the world's game of death and power.

But during the war a German officer was supposed to lay waste the town of Filiatra. The night before this contemplated atrocity, he had a dream in which an old man with a very long white beard forbade him to engage in such wickedness. Sorely disturbed by his dream, he tried to find out if there was such an old man living in the town. Nobody could answer his questions. Quite by chance he went into the local church: there he saw the old man who had haunted his sleep. It was St Haralambos, staring down from the iconostasis. Instantly the officer cancelled his plans; after the war, according to the locals, he came on a pilgrimage every year and lit a candle in honour of the saint who had saved him. Now that he is dead, his children continue to come.

NOTEBOOK, SPRING 1987

Andreas Papandreou, with the economy looking more than usually battered, is engaging, in the neatly distracting way of politicians, in some sabre rattling over the issue of Turkey's 'invasion' of territorial waters. Radio and television speak of nothing else. A blackout is reportedly in force in Athens, and supermarket shelves all over Greece have been stripped bare. Even here flour and rice are in very short supply.

'All this panic,' I remark foolishly, really only thinking aloud.

Yiayia glares at me and then says loftily, '*You* don't know anything about war. Nothing. *I* know all about it, and οι γυναίκες, the women, say they're coming; they'll be here tomorrow.'

Well, I've brought this on myself by failing to keep my big mouth shut, so the pattern of at least seven years persists, with guilt about my privileged life

79

forming a weft for the long, long warps of suffering, of inescapable divisions in experience.

Later, during the Gulf War of 1991, I keep my thoughts to myself.

Yiayia speaks of the Κατοχή, the Occupation, and shakes her head. Her voice trails off as she sits staring, remembering the endless struggle to keep six children fed and clothed.

'We ate *horta*, wild endive, every day of the war and civil war,' says George. And life, death and suffering went on in the village against the backdrop of the global conflict.

Once Aphrodite had to come to the aid of her sister-in-law, who was having a dangerous and painful miscarriage. Somehow they got to a doctor, and Aphrodite held the kerosene lamp for him while he steered instruments through blood to perform a curette. Aphrodite herself had miscarriages and also lost three children. Little Anna had measles and died.

I picture Aphrodite climbing the stairs slowly as yet another labour begins. She goes to her bedroom, the shutters of which open onto a view of waving green and silver grapevines, and a mountain looming close. The midwife, the *mami*, comes eventually but the births are easy enough and Aprodite is always prepared and scrupulously clean: fresh linen, newly made swaddling-bands, old cloths carefully boiled, a bottle of methylated spirits. Not for her the practice of other women, that of throwing a piece of sacking on the floor.

NOTEBOOK, SUMMER 1983

Today Yiayia tells me about her dead babies, twin girls.

'I knew as soon as they were born that there was something the matter with them. They weren't right, they were deformed. They were so bad that we sent for the doctor.' There is a long pause.

'What did he say?'

A breath is drawn in and there is another silence.

'He took one look at them and said, "They're going to die. Baptize them immediately." So we did. But they didn't die immediately, poor little things. Forty days, it took.'

Forty days is a very long time to wait for death. I do not ask whether she endured agonies of suspense during subsequent pregnancies. It is likely that she didn't. It is likely that she left everything in the hands of God. In any case she had to keep on working ceaselessly: there was never the opportunity for the self-indulgence of worry. Nor was there any romanticizing of motherhood.

'George says you were overjoyed at each new pregnancy. Was that really true?'

She gives a wry grin and then chuckles ruefully before replying.

'Men! Of course it wasn't true. But what could I do about it?' She gives progress a passing tribute. 'Nowadays *o kosmos* knows something about such matters. We didn't know a thing.'

Yiayia does not mention this, but family legend has it that her sister Joanna actually plucked up enough courage to suggest to her priest brother-in-law that constant pregnancy and childbirth were killing Aphrodite. She was sharply reprimanded and loftily informed that, if it were God's will, he, Papadimitri, cherished the ambition of having twelve children, one for each of the disciples. It is easy to imagine Joanna subsiding after this announcement. Whether she considered it a prime example of rationalization or evidence of colossal clerical arrogance is not known. In any case, God had other plans, and Papadimitri had to be content with a mere six children.

Life during the war and civil war, although very difficult, was considerably easier than in Athens. There was always milk, there was always *horta*. There was always wine: George remembers his father floating an egg in the barrel. If an area the size of a two-drachma coin showed on the egg, then the sugar content was high enough. Otherwise a small bag of currants was suspended inside the barrel. He also remembers his mother, in an ironic instance of the deprivation brought about by war, making silk dresses for his sisters. No other material was available, so she went through the entire process of silk making herself, first hatching the silkworm eggs in blankets. It was the children's job, and a difficult one, to keep the voracious little creatures constantly supplied with mulberry leaves.

CRETAN NOTEBOOK, SUMMER 1987

Along the road and in Chania, Rethymnon, Heraklion, I make notes. I am not the only one. At the height of the tourist season, Crete seems to be full of people feverishly scribbling, as individual imagination responds

to landscape and history. We, haunted each one of us
by the symbol of the Phaistos Disk, are making a linear journey in space, but a spiral journey in time.

Set down this, set down this: the notebook bulges
with lists, inventories, feeble similes, pale adjectives,
muddled metaphors, all an attempt to spin a frail web
of words, to freeze the moment, to nail history down,
to make it manageable. But in the end, a straight,
spare note seems better.

At Souda Bay I tried to imagine that bright blue sky
filled with black mushroom shapes on a certain day in
1941, tried to imagine the feelings of the German
paratroops as they floated gently downwards, to be
met, not as they had been told, by friendly Cretans,
but by villagers armed with old guns, knives and
sticks, and determined to fight to the death. And I
remember that Stavros, who escaped from Crete,
reached Gytheion in a rowing-boat and took a week to
walk home to this village. Frank, an English friend
who lives in the Peloponnese, tells me of the small boy
who saved allied soldiers, five of them: he stole a boat
on the shores of Messinian Bay and all six managed to
reach Chania; a poet friend meets a prominent Cretan
theologian, who, at the age of eight, had been a runner
for the Resistance, never stirring anywhere without
making sure his cyanide tablet was in his pocket.

And always there were the women.

A yiayia saved her grandchild by flinging herself on
top of him as shells rained on Chania. Women carried
wounded soldiers on their backs; girls tore up their
dowry sheets, their pride and joy, for bandages.
Women fought so ferociously on one occasion that a
German unit fled before them. Women wore uniforms
and were deported to Germany if captured.

Thousands of allied soldiers were hidden on Crete, as well as on the mainland, and were never betrayed. They were fed and sheltered and, in many cases, helped to escape. One young soldier, whose Cretan rescuers stripped him of everything that might identify him to the enemy, returned fifty years later to find his watch, a gold one and a twenty-first birthday present from his mother, carefully stored away waiting for him to return and claim it. Such incidents gleam like gold thread in a shroud among the ghastliness of bombs, bloodshed, bayonet charges and general carnage.

Now, in the war cemeteries of Crete, black-clad old women light candles on the graves of German soldiers, most of whom were as young as eighteen or twenty, chosen because their bones would be strong enough to withstand the shock of the parachute landing. When asked the reason for their visits the women reply, 'They, too, have a mother, and she is far away or dead. We also lost our sons, killed or executed by the Germans. We know how a mother feels. Now, we are their mothers.'

❦

The details from Niko's history book register in the imagination, but the imagination only accepts them because they are documented fact.

During the winter of 1941–42, the population of Athens starved. The occupying forces sent most produce to Italy and Germany. Galloping inflation had the usual effects and the winter was an extremely severe one.

The pictures are there, the words are there: this is not hearsay, exaggerated oral history, folk memory. In Athens, people clad only in sacks and newspapers shuffled along the streets: it was just a matter of time before their corpses were collected. This collection was made every morning, for people literally dropped dead from starvation.

A woman falls to the pavement as if struck by lightning. A man takes a carob from his pocket and gives it to her. She eats like a hungry dog. A 25-year-old man organizes a group of children. These children sift through the rubbish left outside the restaurants patronized by German soldiers. They find potato and onion skins, vegetable roots, bits of torn lettuce, rotten apples, crusts of bread and half-eaten leftovers. The young man appropriates any cigarette butts found among this conglomeration, and then helps the children boil up a dreadful brew in a tin can over a fire of old papers and rubbish.

And suddenly I remember Kosmas, then a medical student, who managed to live on a ration of one slice of bread a day. He used to cut it into three pieces, for breakfast, dinner and tea. I do not know how long he lived like this. Once a day soup kitchens in Athens served soup made from dried beans: perhaps he was helped by one of these. Three hundred thousand people died of starvation that winter. Without the soup kitchen, it has been calculated, approximately one million would have died.

And there was always resistance. Students protested; there were general strikes. The day the students gathered outside the University of Athens and sang the national anthem, they were subjected to an Italian cavalry charge. Heroines of the resistance, some of them very young, died terrible deaths.

Here in Yiayia's village, girls kept local resistance fighters supplied with food. Some of these youths from the next village shot at least one German officer: because of this the whole village was razed. At Kalavryta in 1943 eight hundred men and boys were shot. Women and children were herded into the schoolhouse, which was then set alight. As the women were doing their desperate best to break down doors and windows, a German soldier unlocked a door and set them free. I have often wondered what happened to him. The women then spent fourteen nights digging graves for their husbands and sons with whatever tools they could find.

The conflicting ideologies in the resistance movement eventually plunged Greece into that most horrible and perverse of conflicts, a civil war. T. S. Eliot was referring to another such conflict when he observed, 'The Civil War is not ended; I doubt whether a civil war ever does end.' It is certainly not over in Greece.

Greeks have long memories. Today, now that the Cold War seems finally to have come to an end, now that communism is discredited, there is much loud criticism of those who were communists during the forties and later. But surely it is not too difficult to understand the appeal of an ideology that promised what seemed like the world to people who had nothing? After all, that same ideology had mesmerized and seduced some of the best minds at Cambridge during the thirties. Some historians maintain that the best intellects of a whole generation of British youth went the way of communism at that time.

Anaïs Nin was anti-communist because she thought that communism persecuted 'the imagination and the dream'. It could be argued, however, that the imagination and the dream flourish most often and flower most fully against a background of privilege.

'The disillusioned communist is more bitter than a disillusioned lover. Because politics are so narrow and demand such single-mindedness, the rest of the personality is atrophied,' wrote Anaïs Nin.

The dates, the names:

SEPTEMBER 1941: Formation of EAM, the National Liberation Front.

DECEMBER 1941: Formation of ELAS, the military arm of EAM, the National Popular Liberation Army. Guerilla bands took to the hills in the early summer of 1942.

EARLY 1942: Formation of EDES, the National Republican Greek League, led by General Napoleon Zervas: the most important non-communist resistance group.

FEB/MARCH 1943: EEAM, the Workers National Liberation Front, organized impressive strikes which blocked German plans to draft Greek workers.

SPRING 1943: Formation of EKKA, National and Social Liberation, led by Colonel Dimitros Psarros.

LATE 1943: Formation of the anti-communist Security Battalions, which were particularly active in the Peloponnese. They regarded communists as being more of a threat than the Germans, and were denounced as collaborators by both the British and the exiled Greek government.

The facts are those of classic guerilla warfare: bands of men lived in caves, venturing forth to strike suddenly, swiftly, and often successfully against the Germans. But one fact boded no good for developments after the war: the destruction of the Gorgopotamos viaduct in Lamia on 25

November 1942, which severed supply lines and was a dazzling example of the military potentiality of armed resistance, was the only significant occasion on which ELAS and EDES ever co-operated.

The communists made several concerted attempts to gain power in Greece. The Germans withdrew in October 1944. The Greeks, however, were fighting among themselves before that time, so that the winter of 1943–44 is known as the First Round in the communist attempt to win supremacy in Greece. The fighting of December 1944 became known as the Second Round. Active hostilities in the civil war did not cease until 16 October 1949 with the defeat of the communist forces. There were sporadic incidents for some months afterwards, but more important than these was the legacy of bitterness which would be Greece's for the foreseeable future. Brooding over all these fragmented, patchy attempts at summary are the names of Papandreou, Eden, Churchill and Stalin.

On 5 November 1944 the Minister for the Navy, Panagiotis Kanellopoulos, making his comment on the two days of anarchy which were part of the communist Second Round, wrote:

Η Ελλάδα μας ραγίζει. Ολα τα είχε πάθει, αλλά έμενε ακέραιο το γυαλί της ηθικής ακεραιότητάς της. Είχε γίνει, μάλιστα, κρύσταλλο, το γυαλί αυτό. Τώρα ραγίζει και τούτο. Δεν λέω ποιός είναι υπεύθυνος. 'Οταν η μοίρα φτάνει σε τέτοια τραγικότητα δε ρωτάς πια για ευθύνες.

Greece is cracking. She had suffered everything, but the glass of her ethical integrity remained intact. That glass had certainly become like crystal. Now that, too, is cracking. I do not say who is responsible. When fate comes to such a tragic point, one does not ask about responsibilities.

Kanellopoulos used the metaphor of cracked glass, crystal, to describe Greece's situation at that time. Yiayia would simply have fallen back on the simple expression, *megalo kako*, a great evil. She would have known the names of ELAS, EDES, General Markos, Zervas, Papandreou, Stalin and Churchill. But all these made up the larger pattern: what really concerned her were the individual strands. It is still not clear to me whether she had any real understanding of communism. Oral cultures use language in an aggregative, rather than an analytical way, taking on a load of epithets and viewing any situation from the stance of the epic. In stories and poems they speak and hear of the brave soldier, the beautiful princess, the wicked witch, the evil ogre. Thus, for people like Yiayia, communism was wicked, evil, anti-Church; solely responsible for the grief, pain and sorrow of the civil war, and later, for the παιδομάζεμα, the wholesale kidnapping of children in northern Greece, a catastrophe of unspeakable proportions.

Aphrodite by this time is a mother of six, priest's wife; symbol of correctness, respectability, law and order, and of the conservative, royalist Peloponnese. She is also a good and popular neighbour. Immediately opposite her lives an older woman who has two sons, one who favours the Right, the other the Left. The latter is highly intelligent and widely read. Years of reading and discussion, and a childhood and youth of grinding poverty, have convinced him of the legitimacy of the communist cause: he does not need persuasion or force to join the guerillas.

One day his panic-stricken mother runs across the road to Aphrodite's house. The men of the Security Battalions are coming, they will inevitably search the woman's house, her George's books will be discovered. They will all be punished, if not killed. Aphrodite does not hesitate. 'Bring the books here,' she says immediately, 'and I will hide them.' So the books are brought across the road and hidden somewhere in that old house, ideal for keeping secrets, full of nooks, crannies and unexpected niches as it is. Aphrodite is reasonably confident that her house will not be searched, for it is, after all, the house of a priest. And it is not searched. Yet the fact remains that it could have been, that she took a calculated risk. But she cannot act otherwise, for she is a mother, asking the mother's question, one seemingly as old as time: Is anything, any belief, worth my son's life?

Greek mothers made their gestures against the meaninglessness of the civil war, and against their own sons' senselessness in risking, and ultimately sacrificing, everything for the sake of empty ideology. That idealistic son of Yiayia's neighbour is now dead. Nothing went right after the end of the civil war. He died of heart failure when he was only sixty-five, but in a sense his heart had failed him long before then. He was one of a number of sad, ageing bachelors who sat in the *kafeneion* nearly all day talking to each other, but who also often fell silent and gazed into space, seeing nothing very much, I imagine, except the ruin of the past, bleak visions blurred by time.

In Kalamata there is a photographer who has album after album filled with photographs of young men, eager and alive, who snatched at immortality via the camera before going to the mountains.

History quickens its pace, the known world collapses, snaps. The pieces have to be picked up again and laboriously reconstructed.

A pregnant woman whose husband has been absent overnight goes out into the orchard. It is early morning, the tender part of the day. The cicadas are not yet shrilling, the heat not yet pressing like a weight. She suddenly sees a heap, a shape lying under a tree. It is her husband; his throat has been cut.

A riderless donkey returns home. Family members, sick at heart, tether the animal and start searching. The body of husband and father is eventually found: he has been beaten to death.

A neighbour's house, a whitewashed stone cottage, is only forty years old. Her brother changes sides during the civil war. The punishment for this betrayal is the burning of the house. The younger daughter of the family never marries, for there is now no dowry. She has no home, is without that shelter, protection, sign of achievement and self-affirmation.

In 1944 one thousand, four hundred and fifty men, women and children are shot at the town of Meligalas, Messinia. Many bodies are dumped in a large well.

Aphrodite's own family almost reaches breaking point. In 1948 George is a boy of ten. It is his job to gather firewood for his mother's oven. He wanders a little further afield than usual one day and suddenly finds himself confronted by an armed guerilla, who points his gun at him and questions him roughly. The child is terrified and runs home as soon as he is let go. On the way he meets an old yiayia, a great-aunt. 'Did you see Yannis just now?' she asks. The guerilla is, in fact, George's cousin.

At night the guerillas gather on the mountainside to yell communist propaganda and news of their successes in battle through megaphones to the village below. They also spend a lot of time arranging a display of rocks. These rocks, white against bushes and undergrowth, eventually form the letters Δ.Σ. Δημοκρατικός Στρατός. Democratic Army.

And one final tug, which nearly proves the undoing of the whole family: one day, Papadimitri arrives at the Church of St Nikoloas in order to take a service. He discovers, during his preparations, that essential olive oil is missing. There is only one explanation: the guerillas, hiding in caves in the mountains at the back of the church, have stolen it. Papadimitri is a mild man, a far gentler personality than his wife, according to reports. He is apparently so gentle and pure in spirit that on one occasion, when he goes to visit his confessor, the local bishop, the latter announces that in an ideal world he and his other priests would make confession to Papadimitri. But there is such a thing as righteous indignation and Papadimitri is more than righteously indignant: he is outraged. In a fume he denounces the thieves from the pulpit and predicts that St Nikolaos will strike them all down. He then returns home and begins to realize what he has done. He considers it wise to report the incident to the bishop and apparently travels to Kalamata that same day. The bishop, it seems, is both horrified and worried. Papadimitri has acted bravely but foolishly. The bishop orders him to leave home immediately and to travel to a seminary in Corinth, there to stay for an indefinite period. Of course Papadimitri obeys, and takes his eldest son, Pericles, with him, for it is an opportunity for him to go to school.

Aphrodite very rarely speaks of this period, but it is one marked by loneliness, isolation and fear. In spite of the community of neighbours and family, and they do help, she is essentially alone. Her sister is in Kalamata, her brother has his own six children to look after. Now she has to do everything, and continues to do everything for two years. Sometimes she and her children can hear gunfire.

Aphrodite assumes a courage she certainly does not feel and opens the outside gate to a marauding band of guerillas. She tries to hide the fact that she feels sick with fear. This attempt is made rather easier as soon as she sees some relatives. As in the case of Papadimitri, righteous indignation boils to the surface and she shames them all into leaving, and leaving empty-handed at that. On another occasion she is not so successful: a group batters the outside door down and she is powerless to stop them taking food and oil.

Life is both more and less than we expect. It seems obvious that Yiayia did not want her husband to go, that she was, in a sense, a victim of history. On the other hand, the Greek temperament is a fatalistic one and, especially then, a pessimistic one as well. «Είναι άνδρας,» Yiayia is fond of saying. 'He is a man,' and the subtext reads: his wishes are my commands. This, at least, is the theory. She accepted the situation because she had no choice.

But, paradoxically, Papadimitri's absence allowed her to develop somewhat on a personal level. It would have been very easy for her simply to follow the established routine, to struggle along on the very slender margin of money and produce that she had. George, then aged eleven and the man of the house in the absence of both his father and his elder brother, recalls being deeply impressed when his mother, after careful thought, decided to buy a quantity of olives. This was strange, for she always sold olives if she could. He was also vaguely troubled at seeing cash being handed over. But what Aphrodite was doing was engaging in a mild form of speculation. Olives were actually a means of exchange: soon after this transaction was made, the price of olives went up and stayed up. According to George, Papadimitri would never have taken this sort of calculated risk.

The EAM, according to British historians C. M. Woodhouse and Richard Clogg, improved the lot of the Greek peasant: schools began to operate again, and some villages gained telephone and wireless for the first time. 'Not least of its attractions,' wrote Clogg, 'was its willingness to utilise the talents of women, who, in an essentially patriarchal society, had hitherto been expected to confine themselves to exclusively domestic concerns.'

NOTEBOOK, SPRING 1991

I have been talking to George, yet again, about his mother. I am slowly groping my way towards the notion that people in an oral culture have a different mental set from those who are literate. I have now been able to do some reading on this subject and have discovered that the differences are particularly striking in the case of mental illness. A schizophrenic from an oral tradition is less likely to retreat into himself, into a confused dreamworld; he is more prone to episodes of extreme external confusion, and may well go berserk or run amok.

George warms to this theme. 'Compare the mind to a computer', he says. 'Both minds and computers process data. The data entering a literate person's mind is virtually unlimited; the data entering an oral person's is limited to what he or she can take in through the senses. If that person lives in an isolated place forever, then what happens is just a processing and repetition of tradition, custom and routine, allowing for a modicum of change through natural progress.'

'What effect does that have on your, oh, I don't know . . . emotional security?'

'The less you know, the more secure you feel. I've always said that.'

'But what about the time of the παιδομάζεμα? Wouldn't your mother have felt much more secure if she had known where it was all happening?'

'Yes, I suppose that's true. All she knew was that the communists were kidnapping children and that there were communists here. Those two facts were linked in her mind, and so she was terrified. That was the extent of her logic.'

She had no way then, I added silently, of combating swirling rumour.

Logic is an invention of the Greeks, anyway, made after they had assimilated the alphabet. Literate people favour the syllogism; oral ones the riddle. Oral people do not use deductive processes at all. In Luria's famous work on cognitive development sixty years ago, an illiterate peasant was shown drawings of four objects: an axe, a saw, a log and hatchet, and asked to indicate the odd one out. He chose to dispense with the hatchet because it was not as efficacious in the chopping of wood as the other tools. When it was pointed out to him that three items were tools and one was wood, he said, 'Well, yes, but we still need wood, otherwise we can't build anything.'

Yiayia, according to George, can probably recognize the map of Greece, but would certainly not be able to make much out of the map of Europe; nor has she any knowledge of which countries can be reached by land and which by sea. Later, I discover that, paradoxically, it is the oral person who has a sense of man being at the centre, the navel of the world, while the literate person has imbibed the notion of flatness through different maps and projections.

Yiayia cannot read, write, ride a bicycle or drive a car. She has never worn makeup, stayed in hospital or had an operation. She cannot swim, and has only once been in a boat. She does not possess a clock or watch, and is thus less deluded than people who try to nail time down by reducing it to space.

She can, however, kill rabbits and hens and use up every portion of a pig. She has a huge store of genealogical data, and a sizeable store of *mirologia*, the songs of fate sung at funerals. She can lay out a corpse.

From 1940 to 1949 Greece had been, once again, on a war footing. The old pattern had not changed, had only taken on a deeper hue. It is recorded that the battles of Grammos and Vitsi took place in the summer of 1949. After the democratic army's defeat in both battles, the remnants, approximately five thousand people, together with the communist party leadership, fled across the border to Albania.

Eighty thousand people died during the civil war. Seven hundred thousand, or ten per cent of the population, were refugees. Twenty-five thousand children between the ages of three and fourteen were taken into the Eastern bloc. Twenty thousand people were sentenced for offences against the state; five thousand of these were condemned to death or to life imprisonment.

The Truman Doctrine was a fact of the years after 1947. Yiayia did not know what it was called, but she knew that it meant a certain source of food for the family. 'Too much sugar, though,' she says. 'We were never used to sugar.'

NOTEBOOK, SUMMER 1991

Incidents as George recalls hearing of them:

A guerilla surrenders, but is later shot by a Right-winger before he can be taken to army headquarters. He is buried in a hastily dug grave, and builders working on the church roof swear that he is still alive at the time of his burial. The guerilla had conscripted and virtually kidnapped his own nephew, then only a boy of seventeen and the only male householder in the absence of his father and older brothers. The guerilla had told his sister that this was little more than she deserved, seeing that her husband was fighting for the fascist forces. Later, the shooter himself dies in a car crash in Melbourne.

The guerillas in this area, with no hope of escaping over northern borders, stay in the mountain caves for as long as they can, but give up their miserable way of life one by one. Most are starving; at least one is naked when he surrenders. But there is one man who stays up there for quite a long time; it is obvious that someone in the village is keeping him supplied with food. Then one day his body is discovered, an empty saucepan lying beside it. The strong rumour, persisting to this day, is that the villager, becoming very frightened of discovery, has poisoned this person who has been so dependent on him. 'Wolves don't eat each other,' wrote Nikos Kazantzakis, 'Greeks do.'

A communist refuses to surrender, and lives above a ceiling in a Kalamata house for ten years. During this period of enforced solitude he teaches himself English and French from books smuggled upstairs. Eventually he is able to leave and go to Russia, where he becomes

97

the author of a Greek-Russian dictionary. Now he is back in Greece, leading, as far as is known, a 'normal' life.

George and I meet one of the ex-colonels, one who wielded great power between 1967 and 1974, now free after having served a prison sentence. I do not want to shake his hand, but as we are all wedding guests in church, I am forced to. What is really difficult to cope with is the fact that he seems a benign, grandfatherly figure. George and he chat easily; I shift from one foot to the other. George says afterwards, 'You over-simplify everything. You need to know this man's history. He was a brave resistance fighter whose mother and sister were killed by the communists.'

Aphrodite in 1948 helps at the funeral of her father-in-law, George Bouras, dead at the age of eighty. Aphrodite's own parents are now both dead; her mother-in-law, Evgenia, will live on until 1964, well into her nineties. George Bouras's father, who married late, had fought in Tripolis against the Pasha. And now that man's descendants are fighting each other.

At the vigil all the pomp and dignity of death is in the bare room: the flickering light of the candles, the scent of flowers, the wail of the *mirologia*. The coffin rests on an ornate table, all gilt and glitter; the double-headed eagle of Byzantium forms a candle-holder at one end, and signifies, as nothing else can, the safe and certain place every Orthodox soul occupies in the endless stream of history.

That history moves on: by 16 October 1949 the civil war

is officially over. Papadimitri comes home. Greece is in ruins; somewhere I have read that there was not a bridge left standing in Greece after the civil war. Some villagers stand trial and are exonerated; others receive light sentences and then return to the village to start their old lives again, at least as far as they are able. Every day our neighbour walks past the house of the man who testified against him. It is easy to agree with Penelope Lively, who maintains that all history is the history of wars.

Kyria Ariadne and her husband built their house almost entirely by themselves, making endless trips barefoot, carrying barrels of lime for the house, then together cutting and dressing the stone. After all this struggle, her husband died young and she was left with three children to rear. She worked day and night, as most women did, but with an edge of desperation added by her widowhood.

She lost one son to a nine-year battle with tuberculosis. His photograph sits on the chest of drawers. He was a solemn, good-looking youth. She gazes at his image and is able to flash a gallant smile.

'Death is part of life. *Paithaki mou*,' she says. '*Ti na kanoume*? He was so ill, poor boy, he suffered so much.' The old fingers stroke the frame of the photograph gently. 'It's all so long ago.'

Serious illnesses – malaria, tuberculosis, poliomyelitis, typhus – were also part of life, but tuberculosis was the real scourge of the time. In the old days, sufferers were taken to live in shepherd's huts. Their families would leave them food to be collected from a safe distance. Wealthier victims were able to rest in relative comfort in the mountains, the higher the better. Girls who recovered from tuberculosis never mentioned the illness, for nobody wanted to marry a person so tainted.

'I knew my son would die,' states Kyria Ariadne matter-of-factly, 'because of a dream I had had. Ach, it is still so real to me, this dream. There were three birds sitting on the rafters in my house. A canary, a rooster and a dove, and they all had wings that were drooping mournfully. When I went towards the canary and the dove, they shrank away. But not the rooster. When I went to him, he struck me four times with his wings. And I awoke in great fear, because I knew that four deaths would follow. And they did: four deaths in the family, and my son's was one of them.'

NOTEBOOK, SPRING 1991

In the mountains there is a little bird, the τσοπανάκο, which follows the flocks of sheep and goats and likes the company of shepherds. He owes his existence, this little bird, to forgetfulness, magic and punishment. Once upon a time there was a shepherd boy who became so engrossed in the game he was playing that he completely forgot his sheep. The whole flock wandered away, far into the mountains, where they were eaten by wolves. In deep shame and cursed by the mother of mothers, the child turned into the τσοπανάκο bird, and as that bird he now follows the flocks and whistles like the real shepherd he once was, seeking his lost sheep.

Fairies are τα πονηρά πνεύματα, the cunning spirits. Fairy women are ethereal creatures veiled in cobwebs. They dance in villages at night. If, in times gone by, they ever found anybody asleep on the threshing floor, they caused him to become deaf, mute and paralysed. But such people could hear fairy songs and music forever after.

Behind the village, somewhere very high up, there is a fairies' garden. It is not a quiet place, for it is haunted by sound, that of women washing and beating clothes night and day. Grasses from the fairies' garden are certain protection against snakebite, but those who draw near to the place feel as if they are being dragged and pushed, and usually fall to their hands and knees and break out in a cold sweat, at the mercy of some great power or strange magnetic field.

Papadimitri learned the bitter lesson that man's faith in God can be severely tested, and faith in one's fellow man can be entirely destroyed. He believed that there are such things as fairies. So did most villagers, even though a rational explanation often followed sightings. A devil sitting on the cemetery wall proved to be, in the morning light, a goat peering over that same wall. The noise that accompanied George as he wore a pair of velvet trousers courtesy of American aid was not, as he had first feared, the sound of little people dogging his footsteps, but that of the nap rubbing as he walked. There have been sightings of fairies riding broomsticks, and fairies are always abroad at midday during the summer months: one must be very careful where one takes a siesta. Fire and light are weapons against fairies, as they are against the *kallikantzaroi*, the spirits of the dead who roam the earth during the twelve days of Christmas.

NOTEBOOK, SPRING 1992

Stories my neighbour tells me. I think, not for the first

time, how it seems to be the women who guard the
myths, legends, customs, traditions, spells, herbal
recipes, tales of fairies and ghosts, the swirling mass
that is part of religion: the stories of weeping icons,
miracles, amazing conversions, tragic martyrs.

'There was once a man called Kiprianos, who had
amazing magical powers and was, as a consequence,
very famous. The king fell in love with a beautiful
girl, a girl as fair and pure as a lily, and wanted to
marry her, but she was set on becoming a nun. In desperation the king went to Kiprianos and asked him to
cast a spell or use a love potion to make this exquisite
creature fall in love with him. He was determined to
have her, you see. But every time Kiprianos and his
attendant devils tried to work their magic, the girl
used the sign of the cross as a highly effective weapon,
and so nothing happened. Finally Kiprianos's curiosity
overcame him, and he wanted to know about this
power higher and stronger than his own. Eventually he
was convinced, converted and baptized. And to show
the public his sincerity, he burnt all his books of spells
and all his recipes for potions in the market-place.'

'But, Vivi,' I ask, 'what happened to the king and
the girl?'

'I don't know. Nothing, I imagine. That's not the
point of the story.

'What I'm going to tell you now happened just
recently. A bus-driver was taking a party of people on
an εκδρομή, an excursion, and they all wanted to stop
at a particular church to light a candle and pay their
respects to a famous icon. The driver moaned and protested. He wasn't a religious man, he didn't want to
stop. No doubt he was thinking of his dinner and his
κρασάκι. But he did stop and the passengers all

102

streamed into the church. He closed the bus and
started reluctantly in their wake. And then . . . and
then . . . he was struck down in the middle of the
road.'

'What do you mean, struck down?'

'Just what I say. He fell in a heap, just like that,
fully conscious and absolutely unable to move.'

'What happened then?'

'The passengers had to get the priest, who brought
the *Evangelio* out of the church and read it aloud over
the bus-driver. It wasn't very long before he was able
to get up, was just as good as new and quite able to
drive. But what a lesson! He won't dare complain, ever
again, about having to stop at a church.'

'I should think not.'

'Now, before you go you must hear this about
Chios. Pirates attacked a monastery there and slaught-
ered all the monks.'

'When?'

'I don't know exactly. Why is it so important? Let
me go on. Only one altar boy was saved and that was
because he called on the saint of the monastery to rescue him. Naturally the saint heard his cry and put the
boy up on the roof out of harm's way. Immediately all
danger was past, the boy wanted to paint an icon of
the saint, but he had no paint and was not an artist.
Clenching his fists in frustration he drew blood, which
then gave him the idea of collecting all the blood of
the murdered monks and mixing it with white clay. So
that's how he was able to mould the face and figure of
the saint.'

'Ugh, Vivi!'

'What's the matter? Do you know that the atmosphere of this church is still so charged that people feel

cold on the hottest day, and unbelievers are stopped in their tracks?'

'I don't wonder at it.'

Later I ask Yiayia what she thinks of Vivi's stories.

'She knows a lot, Vivi.'

'I know what I can recall,' wrote W. J. Ong.

The years after the civil war were hard ones. The economy was shattered, the people exhausted. Between 1946 and 1952 there were sixteen different administrations. The United States aided but also kept a very watchful eye on Greece; a million US dollars a day was poured into the Greek economy. It is also on record that the Left continued to be harassed and that certification of 'healthy social views' was necessary for employment as a public servant, the issue of a driver's licence or passport, and, temporarily, for university entrance. Vast systems of dossiers on the political views, leanings and aspirations of hundreds of thousands of Greeks were built up.

Nineteen fifty-two was the first year of eleven years of right-wing rule, which at least had the effect of enabling some sort of economic progress to be made.

NOTEBOOK, SPRING 1991

We have many visitors, many Australian visitors. Yiayia takes great interest in meeting them all, the more so as she has been to Australia herself. Recently I introduced her to two Australian women of about my own age. Both are tall and statuesque in build; both are mothers of daughters. Yiayia was enchanted by them.

'What beautiful women. And they have daughters.'

All Yiayia's daughters-in-law have produced sons. 'Everybody wants boys, that is only natural, but couldn't one of you have produced a daughter, so that my name could live on?' So she reasons.

'What strong beautiful women. Look how tall and well made they are! Not like you, you poor, short, skinny little thing.'

I huffed and puffed in great indignation. 'I am not skinny. And you're shorter than I am!'

'Never mind that. That doesn't matter. Aren't they lovely?' The paean continued indefinitely.

'What all this means, of course,' said one friend thoughtfully, 'is that your mother-in-law assesses women, at least on a first meeting, in terms of their ability to work, and to work hard. Now you, you're not really built for physical labour.'

The work went on and on. Work to support a son at school, for in 1950 George started secondary school in Kalamata. Work to provide a certain amount of cash for the daughters' dowries.

The need to provide a dowry was a pressing one. The Papandreou government of the 1980s abolished the dowry, but the custom still prevails and will do so for a generation or two yet. As late as 1981 my youngest sister-in-law told me in a matter-of-fact way that no girl could hope to get a good husband unless she had a sizeable dowry. For his daughters, Papadimitri sold precious land; Aphrodite prepared the trousseaux. There is no evidence to suggest that she resented the hours of effort involved, but resentment was obviously felt by other women; resentment, but also acknowledgement of the inevitability of accepting the responsibility. Both aspects have been expressed in song:

> I have a daughter and I have a bitterness
> I will be weaving night and day
> I have a daughter and I have sorrow
> They will be demanding me to provide a house
> I have a daughter and I have troubles
> I have to get up at dawn and sleep at midnight.

Vasso married her third cousin and went to live on the corner opposite her parents' house. The year was 1956: she was the eldest daughter, a fragile beauty. In village terms, hers was an ideal match. She still lives on the corner, although the old house she lived in as a newly-wed has long gone, replaced by a large, modern and very comfortable dwelling. Her parents were delighted that they did not lose her to a stranger, delighted that she moved a mere fifty metres away from her original home. And now Vasso does what she has always done, which is pass her days in an endless round of household tasks and in caring for goats, hens and rabbits. Her life is very like the one her mother led, except that it is a more comfortable one because of social change and an undreamed of prosperity.

Village women, and indeed all Orthodox, put the Panagia, the Mother of God, first in their prayers. Through the Mother of God and her power, women are transformed from wilful, wicked Eves into honourable pillars of home, church and family. The man establishes the house, but the woman is responsible for the physical and spiritual order of it. The state of her house reflects a woman's moral character, as does the fact that she spends a large part of her day cooking. The average village woman, even today, has a deep distrust of short cuts in cooking, and a horror of fast food. The act of cooking is many layered: the produce of the fields is turned into food in an act of cultural transformation, while cooking nurtures the family and is a symbol of love. Food can even be seen to mediate between this world and the next: boiled wheat is eaten at the memorial services for the dead.

As the eldest daughter and eldest child, Vasso helped raise her five brothers and sisters, often looking after them while her parents worked in the olive groves. She went on to raise three children of her own. Now she is a grandmother and the wheel has come full circle, as she is Yiayia's prop and mainstay in the latter's old age.

Village women, and not only village women, like to feel that powerful men are looking after them. In the case of traditional women this feeling often spreads further than the domestic situation, involving father or husband, into politics. They fervently and naturally desire to be protected from war, death, poverty and starvation.

Once, Yiayia, during a rare conversation about politics, padded upstairs, went directly to the specific *baoulo*, and extracted a roll of paper from its depths. Downstairs, she proudly revealed the roll to be a large photograph of Karamanlis.

«Νάτος,» she said, simply. 'Here he is. He's the one for me. Πάρα πολή καλός. He's very, very good.'

In 1955 there are violent anti-Greek riots in Instanbul in reaction to Cyprus's moves towards independence. Field Marshal and Prime Minister Papagos dies in 1955. King Paul asks Konstantine Karamanlis to form a government. Picture the ribbon of history unrolling and Karamanlis becoming one of Greece's most respected statesmen, as great, some say, as Venizelos. But Karamanlis's personal history is troubled. In ancient times, Pericles maintained that the man who took no part in politics was not merely unobtrusive but useless. At least Karamanlis, despite later loneliness and exile, has the satisfaction of knowing that he is of use.

Elections were scheduled for February 1956. Women were to vote for the first time. In the old days, whenever a boy was born, people used to say, 'That's another vote.' In the Mani they said instead, 'That's another pistol.'

The fifties and sixties saw the resurgence of the Left and increasing violence on Cyprus. In 1960 Cyprus was declared an independent republic within the then British Commonwealth of Nations. Enosis, the movement for union with Greece, had apparently ended. Karamanlis had a vision of Greece in Europe: he began a program aimed at the development of tourism; he was pro-NATO and wanted Greece to become a member of the infant EEC. Overall standards of living were rising in Greece, but inequalities in the distribution of wealth continued to grow. During these years the population of Athens grew apace as the centralizing trend continued. This trend began as country dwellers sought, often mistakenly, safety during the years of the civil war. Notions of an expanding middle class, of upward social mobility, seemed applicable for the first time.

Life in the countryside became slightly easier in a material sense, and very much easier on a deeper level as the mental and emotional strain of the civil war years gradually receded. On the surface, the family life of Aphrodite and Papadimitri did not change a great deal: the routine of work in primitive conditions still continued. The house did not acquire running water in the kitchen until 1975; there was no bathroom until 1977.

But change was about to occur. While Vasso had married within the village, Pericles met and chose to marry Efthemia, from Volos in northern Greece. This union signalled a breaking of a centuries-old pattern. As it happened, only the second daughter, Aspasia, married within the village, and she, too, moved away to Athens, then a kind of Mecca for country girls who wanted to escape the drudgery and grind of the rural round.

Efthemia's father was a refugee from Asia Minor; he had seen both his brothers shot during the exchange of populations in 1922. There seemed nothing for him to do but start again in a difficult present. He married and produced three children but died comparatively young. Towards the end of his life he would sit and weep, recalling his lost brothers, one of whom had been shot as he broke away, desperate with thirst, from a refugee column.

For the engagement Aphrodite sets off on her first long journey. She has never even been to Athens before and now she must travel eight hundred kilometres alone. Papadimitri does not go to Volos; it is too far and the house and animals cannot be left. Aphrodite, nervous, agitated, gets everything ready; raps out orders, organizes everybody, asserts authority, which is what she always does when life and circumstances do not follow a predictable pattern.

She sets off by bus, with suitcase and numerous bundles and boxes, for country people always make gifts of produce to city dwellers: heaps of *horta*, globes of *myzithra* (cottage cheese), containers of local olives pickled in brine. She leaves with trepidation in her heart at the prospect of meeting her first daughter-in-law, for she has to accept this situation as one quite outside her experience. She has not been supervisor of the courtship, she does not know the bride or the bride's family. She has not been able to attend the *faneromata* – the ritual revealing of the match.

Aphrodite sets off into the unknown.

There is also the whole dynamic of the mother-in-law/daughter-in-law relationship to be considered, although not, of course, openly. Mothers-in-law expect to be dominant, but this daugher-in-law is not a village girl; she is a city girl who has had a job, who has finished school, who has a parent from across the water, from that sophisticated place, Asia Minor. She is a northerner: that old north-south divide operates in Greece as it does in Italy. And it develops that this daughter-in-law has a personality as strong as Aphrodite's, as strong as her new husband's. There will be many a clash, but she will not be cowed, will remain her own person.

In the wedding photograph, Efthemia is smiling confidently in her doyley dress of many layers and much beading, beside a mustachioed, handsome Pericles. By that time Aphrodite has left them, the newly-weds, to their life in suburbia and returned to the village where Pericles will never live again, and where Efthemia spends, she says later, one night and one night only.

During the sixties there developed signs of lack of confidence on the part of the Right. It was alleged that the 1961 elections were rigged. George Papandreou's cry referred to 'the relentless struggle' to get new elections.

In May 1963 Left-wing deputy Dr Gregory Lambrakis was assassinated by ultra-Right-wing thugs at a peace rally in Thessaloniki. Links were suspected between the assassins and highly placed state officials. Later, Michael Cacoyannis made the film *Z*, based on this incident: it was to become internationally famous.

On 11 June Karamanlis, totally disillusioned with the Greek political system, resigned. He travelled into self-imposed exile in Paris, where he remained for eleven years.

In February 1964 George Papandreou had a decisive win in the elections. The sixties were also the years of a great migration wave to Australia and elsewhere. During the twenty years from 1950 to 1970, nine hundred thousand people left Greece. Melbourne eventually became the third largest Greek-speaking city in the world and remains so today. Chicago, of course, has a larger Greek population, but time and the removal of generations from the *patritha* mean that comparatively few young Greek-Americans speak Greek.

NOTEBOOK, WINTER 1991

Widowhood and emigration are, it is said, metaphors for death, with stations and airports being rehearsals of that final separation. Yiayia has suffered as a result of both.

Remembering Hellmut, whom I met in the Melbourne of the seventies. 'Hitler taught me I was a Jew,' he used to say. His family had lived in Prussia for more than three centuries; in 1938 he, his wife and two children escaped from Germany and went, eventually, to Australia. He knew of the inexorability of history and of the impotence of education, culture, even of civilization, against evil men and a certain combination of circumstances and events. He would weep over his memories, but his sadness would take on a cynical tone as he pondered the folly of mankind: 'They said it couldn't happen in the land of Goethe and Schiller. Ha!' And the bitter chuckle would hang in the air.

Now young people choose to move away, especially from here. Old people left, most often, because dire need forced them to. Young people leave because they are irked by the restrictions of small-town life, view the village atmosphere as one geared to control, consider the black-clad yiayiathes members of a highly efficient network of spies. They must leave in order to learn that they can never do so: the village will be with them always.

It may take a few years, but they eventually learn, even if not consciously, that while on one level they reject the village, on another, deeper, level they are bound to it in ways they cannot, or do not wish to, explain. And so they return for Christmas, for Pascha, for the summer holidays. I, only an observer, always on the edge of things, can see the authority a sense of place exercises over them, the way it has them all in thrall.

Yiayia's world used to have a radius of a few kilometres. Now that radius has been reduced to only a few hundred metres as she shuffles between her own house, her daughter's and her son's. She refers to people from a village two kilometres away as foreigners.

'What does that make me?' I tease her on one occasion.

She grins at me, eyes wrinkling. 'That's different. You're different. You're ours.'

With Efthemia at a funeral. We are standing in the village churchyard and, after the coffin has been lowered into the grave, she turns to me and says, with a sigh behind her wry smile, 'Where are they going to bury us, the foreigners?'

There is a tradition that the Panagia, the Mother of God, was travelling with St John the Evangelist when they were

112

forced to rest in the area of Mt Athos because of a storm at sea. Now this area is called the Orchard of the Panagia. Why was she travelling?

I had a shocking dream once. I have never forgotten it. I am trapped in Yiayia's house with Dimitrios and Nikolaos, who are only little. There is no way out: all doors and windows seem to have disappeared. A monster appears, in the way of dreams, quite without warning. It is large, dark and hairy, and walks on all fours. Its nether lip is truly horrible to look at: glistening, red and drooping. I try, protecting my children, to show a bravery I do not feel.

'What are you, anyway?' I say in what I hope are challenging tones. 'A bear? What?'

The thing looks at me, snorts threateningly and then growls, 'I'm a foreigner.'

Glenda Adams, on living in New York: 'And I loved the life I was leading there, pottering around that city, where there is no prescribed way to live your life, where you can find your own group and unearth a confidence and aspects of your personality that could well remain hidden or latent in the smaller society at home.'

In cities there is indeed no prescribed way to live life; in villages and townships, no matter where they are, there nearly always is, which is why people often choose to leave them. A foreigner marooned in a village discovers that there is often only one group; if one cannot be a part of it, for whatever reason, all confidence eventually evaporates and many aspects of the personality become atrophied. Sense of self is drastically impaired; in extreme cases even sanity is threatened. But of course it takes one years and years to realize what is happening. For a person born to village life, however, and then forced to leave it, the prescriptions and the familiar security are yearned for, often quite desperately. We can only be, any of us, what we are.

George migrates, like Kyria Yannoula's husband, like his uncles, because he is discouraged. He cannot afford to finish his polytechnic course. His job as a purchasing officer does not pay at all well, and there is no prospect of advancement. Pipitsa, his youngest sister, will soon need a dowry. The Church and the Australian government are sponsoring the migration program, and two of his friends from the village have already left. He, too, leaves, and does not know, fortunately, that he will never see his father again.

Yiayia weeps in the olive groves, and twenty-five years later, when my own son emigrates, says, 'Don't cry too much, παιδάκι μου. It doesn't do, really it doesn't.' And we stare at each other across a chasm of time and cultures, united, against all the odds, in that apparently endless repetition of separation and reunion. For both George and Dimitri come back, do not disappear forever.

But then I did not know when, or if, Dimitri would be back. I am not brave, not at all, and do not cope well with separations. I cried a lot and went for long, solitary walks. Grief is a strange, uncontrollable thing, and I have often thought that grieving for the living is worse than grieving for the dead. That's the effect of hope, I suppose.

I torture myself by dwelling on Dimitri's ignorance of the Australian environment: surf, sharks, spiders, the bush, the big bad cities. He is simply not Australian, my son; he will have to learn, perhaps the hard way, how to fit in. As for myself, I am not the little Aussie battler I am supposed to be. I think of my own traditions while walking in this foreign land and manage to raise a rueful laugh. Ned Kelly instructed the hangman to tell them he died game;

Breaker Morant told the British firing squad to 'shoot straight, you bastards'. Australians worship courage in defeat, and I can show none. Disgraceful, really, for at least I can write letters.

From 1965 until 1972 Aphrodite is dependent, for news of George, on Papadimitri's writing of a monthly letter and his reading aloud of the reply.

NOTEBOOK, WINTER 1991–92

In Australia George always felt a foreigner; now Australian-born Dimitri does not know how he feels. Back in the village at Christmas-time he is culture-shocked.

'God, what a place. How can you bear it, Mum? Nothing ever happens, and nobody ever *wants* anything to happen.'

Eight weeks later it was: 'Mum, I don't want to go. I'm sick of this two countries business. Why can't I decide? I want to settle.'

'Heavens, Dimitri. Very few people are settled at the age of nineteen. Anyway, think of how well you fit into both places. Not like me. I don't belong anywhere any more. You say you don't want to go, but you don't want to stay, either, do you?'

'No, I don't.'

And still later he writes, 'I don't know. Life in Greece seems so simple.'

I seize pen and paper almost immediately and write back, '*Never* think that life in Greece is simple.'

Perhaps he'll learn, I tell myself, when he starts his history course, that life, like history, is invariably complicated – and messy.

History sometimes suggests simplicities, but such simplicities are not always desirable.

History records the existence of the Aspida conspiracy, and then the colonels' coup of 21 April 1967. Once again the knot had come to the comb. The colonels' motivation, according to analysts of these events, was that they feared an imminent takeover by the communists; but, other experts say, there was never any evidence to suggest that this might happen.

Historian Richard Clogg asserts that the conspirators' real fear was that a centre union victory in elections would have been followed by a purge of officers of known ultra-Right-wing views. This fear was compounded by a strong feeling that officers had been largely passed over during the consumer boom of the 1960s. And so the colonels came to power and remained in what appeared to be an unassailable position for seven years.

A counter-coup attempted by King Constantine on 13 December 1967 was a failure and the young monarch and his wife and family fled into exile. Today they live in England and are still not permitted to return to Greece.

NOTEBOOK, WINTER 1992

George says that the colonels' motto struck a chord: «Ελλάς, Ελλήνων, Χριστιανών.» 'Greece for Greek Christians.' «πατρίδα, θρυσκεία, οικογένεια.» 'Fatherland, religion, family.'

Papandreou the elder retorted, «Ελλάς ελλήνων Χριστιανών καθολικων διαμαρτηΧωμένων.» 'Greece for Greek Christians united in protest' – a very clever pun in Greek, including, as it does, references to both Catholics and Protestants.

'Things were organized, neat and tidy when the

colonels were around,' remembers Yiayia. 'We weren't allowed to throw our wash-up water into the gutter. Girls wore uniforms to school and behaved respectably. You never heard the language you hear, *I* hear, nowadays.'

Most people in the countryside welcome simplicity, are wary of complexity. They also welcome stability, and in 1967 did not actually notice too much difference in their daily lives. They had not seen the tanks rolling through Athenian streets before dawn on that day in 1967. What rural people did know was that peasants' debts had been abolished.

The colonels, so it seemed, were intent on improving the pattern that Metaxas had tried to weave. There was much the same emphasis on the glory of ancient Greece and on the Christian tradition of Byzantium. The need to discipline the essentially wayward individuality of the Greek character was emphasized. The peasants' interests were looked after: roads were built and water put on in remote villages.

But it is now known that the regime was even harsher than it appeared after the implementation of the 1968 constitution, a document which gave the military enormous control. Its role, according to historian Richard Clogg, was to safeguard the independence and territorial integrity of Greece, 'together with the existing political and social order'.

After 1974 dreadful details emerged of prisons, beatings, torture and illegal confinements – the dark underbelly of the simplicities and certainties that the peasant soul, and not only the peasant one, so craved. Many intellectuals, artists and liberal politicians had exile forced upon them:

for Greeks such as these the wait of seven years must have seemed interminable. Everywhere they waited: in America, Canada, Australia, Britain and France, writing, playing and composing the music of protest, operating pirate radio stations, organizing and attending meetings, lobbying liberal politicians of whichever country they were living in.

On 22 April 1967 George felt completely cut off from Greece. Every Greek in Melbourne had apparently heard rumours of a coup, but all attempts to contact Greece by phone failed completely.

It was later learned that the colonels had, predictably, severed contact with the outside world. When news did begin to filter through, it was difficult to assess. And later, reports, again predictably, laid great stress on the colonels' visions and plans. There was deep gratitude for the fact that the coup had apparently been bloodless: a long time elapsed before Melbourne's Greeks realized the truth about the colonels' extremely authoritarian regime. George himself did not return to Greece for over ten years, going back for a holiday in 1975. By that time everything in Greece had changed once more.

How to describe, capture, annotate the years between 1967 and 1972? How, once more, to deal with the fact that Aphrodite's life is one in which nothing happens and everything happens? There are no passionate love affairs to record, no dramatic changes in mid-life or career, just the small, steady changes and the accumulation of loss, but also gain, which every parent expects.

By 1971 Aphrodite and Papadimitri were in their early sixties; all their children had left home and four of the six were married. Pipitsa, the youngest, married in April 1971 and went to live in Athens. The youngest son, Nikos, had attended the local high school; he, too left for Athens in order to do an engineering course. His life had been made easier by the establishment of the local secondary school: not for him the early separation and hardship of leaving home for the sake of gaining an education.

So time slipped by, almost unnoticeably, but inexorably. More grandchildren were born, a source of both pleasure and status. Each year was marked by the autumn grape harvest, the winter olive harvest, the spring plantings, the summer matings of the animals, the church's holy days, birth and death. The basic lifestyle was essentially a medieval one, with the seasons imposing the age-old pattern of feast and fast. The facts were, as ever, those of life and death, with food and drink representing survival on one level, community and celebration on another. Food and drink symbolized social and religious victory over suffering.

In 1966 television came to Greece but Aphrodite and Papadimitri did not buy a set. What they ever thought of the decisive events and trends of our times I do not know. Korea, the Hungarian revolution, the arms race, the space race, the dismantling of empires; wars in Algeria, Vietnam and the Middle East; the Prague Spring – all this seems to have passed them by. But Papadimitri would have followed developments in Cyprus in 1971: the return of Grivas and the guerilla campaign against Makarios. Television's parade of instant history, the shrinking of the globe into a village, must have come too late. They had witnessed the birth of the modern world without quite realizing it.

Perhaps they did not want to know too much, anyway. Their lives had been so subject to chance and the movements of history that they must have preferred to ignore the outside world whenever possible. They themselves certainly did not want to initiate any changes in an established routine. The notion that restrictions bring freedom from anxiety is a powerful one and always has been: there is often no desire even to test or strain against the boundaries of a received life. And it is a privilege, in a way, not to have to justify the work you do or the way you live, to know you are right in your efforts, not to be pulled in different directions; to be quite certain that, as long as you are able to continue living your contented traditional life, the outside world is largely irrelevant.

But theirs was very possibly the last generation able to live in this way. That sense of wholeness, of completeness has been badly eroded.

In 1972 Aphrodite and Papadimitri had been married nearly forty-one years. If they were not in love at the time of their wedding, it seems likely that love, for want of a better word, grew during the course of the marriage. Perhaps this overstates the case, but they are remembered as having been contented together, as complementary personalities often are.

In Greece the cuckoo is the herald of death, and one called long and monotonously on the night Papadimitri died: 28 February 1972. Papadimitri himself apparently had not been aware that he was ill, although a doctor acquaintance, meeting him by chance in Kalamata one day, knew immediately that he had not long to live. And nurse Katie, years later, looking at the family albums, suddenly bent close over photographs of a young Papadimitri and an old one and said, 'Your father-in-law died of cancer of the pituitary gland, didn't he?'

The story is not told often, but the bare outlines are these: Papadimitri conducted services as usual on Sunday, felt unwell early in the week, and was admitted to a Kalamata clinic so that tests could be made. He died at some stage during that first night, and Pericles had to make the trip from Kalamata to the village in order to tell his mother.

120

He caught her at the outside door of the house, just as she was setting off to the bus-stop.

Aphrodite, dressed in the black she would wear from then on, sat stunned with shock in the best room of the house, which had had the white filet upholstery hastily changed. Near this room was the office Papadimitri would never use again: later Aphrodite cleared it of his books and papers and it became her bedroom. The oil-lamp, the *kandili*, burned beneath a collection of icons; Papadimitri's photograph gazed from the wall. Did Aphrodite sing the *mirologia*, or simply listen to her daughters and sisters-in-law? They sang of Papadimitri's good character and loving ways, of the exemplary life he had led as husband, father and priest. He had been greatly loved. He had seen all his children married or engaged, settled and happy. His life's work was done.

NOTEBOOK, SPRING 1991

Remembering the cloud of depression that settled on George before he even knew of his father's death: that cloud is the strongest proof I have ever seen or experienced of the power of one soul to take farewell of another. A phone call simply confirmed what he already knew to be true.

'To love,' wrote Marianne Wiggins, 'is to accept that one might die another death, before one dies one's own.'

Much later, a conversation with Yiayia: 'It was terrible when the children left home, terrible. But worse than that is being left alone, quite alone.' And she slaps her knee and stamps her foot in a gesture I have never fully understood: an odd mixture of protest and resignation?

She has been a widow for twenty years.

> The widow stays inside the house
> > – gossip around her all around
> The widow stays inside the house
> > – gossip around her all around
> > (Painful exile!)
> She can't gaze out the window, she can't sit by the
> doorstep
> > (Bitter widow)
> There are fresh breezes by the window, there is gay
> chatting by the doorstep.
> > (Bitter widow)
> Widow, go change your name, don't let them call
> you widow!
> > (Ah, bitter widow)
> Widow, night comes on the mountains, yet soon
> daylight sets in.
> > (Bitter widow)
> But so many plumes and feathers as a black hen has,
> > (Bitter widow)
> So many times must you sit and wait at your front
> door, my widow.
> > (Ah, bitter woman)

After Papadimitri's death the frail communication between Greece and Australia was broken for Yiayia, and for George. It is difficult to know exactly what the lack of communication meant to Yiayia, but much easier to know what it meant to George. He worried about his mother and about the loneliness of her widowhood; he worried about his own loneliness now that he did not hear from her. From this time on all his energies were directed toward persuading her to visit him in Australia.

CHAPTER FIVE
JOURNEY AND RETURN

*There is therefore a secret glome or bottom
of our days . . . there is therefore some other
hand that twines the thread of life than that
of Nature.*
Religio Medici, *Sir Thomas Browne*

In the distant land of Phrygia the oracle told the citizens that peace would return to their warring country when they made a king of the first man they met approaching the temple of Zeus in a wagon. This man was the peasant Gordius, who dedicated his ox-cart to Zeus and joined the yoke and pole of the cart in a peculiar, intricate knot of his own invention. The legend grew that whoever untied it would become lord of Asia. Alexander the Great, a man with no time to spare, slashed the knot apart with his sword. The moral of the story is that the power of the sword was proved, in at least that case, to be mightier than that of a deeply revered religious mystery.

To cut the Gordian knot: to get out of a difficult position by means of one decisive step.

After February 1972 George felt increasingly that his position was a very difficult one. He was not where he wanted to be. He was desperately homesick and missed his mother. She in her turn was finding, once the first grief and shock had passed, the adjustment to widowhood a tedious and unhappy process. There seemed no particular reason to follow the old routine now that she was alone. She did, however, follow it – instinctively, for she knew no other, and at a deeper level she probably sensed that such structures get us all through the hardest moments of the hardest days.

Eventually she decided that a break in routine would do her good. She allowed herself to be persuaded. George sent her the money for an air ticket and she decided to visit Melbourne in December 1973.

In November of that year Nikos had married in the ancient city of Thebes. Now all Aphrodite's children were settled.

History cannot forget November 1973 either. On the seventeenth of the month students at the Athens Polytechnic rose in revolt, took over the buildings, and began broadcasting from their pirate radio. University of Athens students had already made a similar effort at protest in March of the same year, and had failed. The polytechnic uprising was put down with great severity. Thirty-four people – students and their supporters – were killed, several hundred wounded, and almost a thousand arrested. Many were, as can be imagined, very young. Such actions had the natural effect of arousing widespread revulsion.

For Papadopoulos, the leader of the military regime, the end had come. The army, with the support of air force and naval units, deposed him in a bloodless coup. Real power now rested with Dimitrios Ioannides, who was commander of the military police, a body which had developed a shocking reputation for brutality towards the regime's opponents. This new regime, however, proved incapable of dealing with the many problems besetting both it and the country.

After these events, which are never mentioned by Aphrodite, she fusses over her packing, delegates all her household tasks, care of the goat and donkey, vegetable garden and olive groves to Vasso, and catches the bus to Athens. She starts the longest journey of her life, and once more she is setting off to meet a daughter-in-law for the first time, this one even more foreign than the one from northern Greece. She takes presents for George; a bottle of ouzo and a length of homemade sausage. Thirty hours later she is most irate when customs officials at Tullamarine confiscate the latter offering.

Inside the capsule of steel which will somehow, she cannot understand how, get her to the other end of the world in an amazingly short time, she does not know what the air-hostesses are doing when they hand out heated towels. In her mental landscape and time-scale, Kalamata is still three hours' donkey ride away, even though the bus service has whittled that time down to a mere half-hour. She is seated next to an older Cypriot woman who is even more bewildered than she is. This woman, also a villager, has so little idea of modern travel that she thinks all her property must be absolutely portable: she is wearing seven black skirts and can hardly fit into the aeroplane seat. What a peasant, thinks Aphrodite.

Aphrodite's seat has a view of the plane's wing, although she does not realize this. Glancing out the window she notices what she knows are letters painted some distance below her. Feeling nervous, she settles into her seat, makes the sign of the cross several times, Η Παναγία μας με φιλαεί, shuts her eyes and crosses her arms and legs. Time passes, she feels strange movements and sensations but does not open her eyes. When she finally decides to do so, she is mightily amazed to see the same letters below her: she is quite sure that the plane is still sitting on the tarmac at Athens airport.

It is Christmas Day 1973. The plane is late. When at last it arrives, George is craning his neck and waving through the constantly opening and closing doors of the Tulla-marine arrivals hall. Inside, a short woman with steel-grey hair and wearing deep black is waving back. Later she tells us that the old Cypriot woman asks, as she peers through the doors and tries to follow the path of Yiayia's gaze, 'Which one is your son?'

The reply comes without hesitation. 'The most beautiful one, of course!'

A Greek story: Mother Partridge and Mother Owl were going to the local school in order to give their children some lunch. Mother Partridge was a busy bird and asked Mother Owl whether she would mind giving the food to Master and Miss Partridge.

'I don't mind at all,' said the obliging owl, 'but I don't know your children.'

'You'll know them immediately,' replied the proud partridge, 'because they will be the most beautiful children to be seen in the schoolyard.'

But some time later Mother Owl brought the food back to Mother Partridge.

'I'm sorry,' she said, simply. 'I couldn't find your offspring. The most beautiful children in the schoolyard were my own.'

Tearful reunion, wary introduction. Sitting in the back seat of the car on my way home, ears and Greek at full stretch, I hear Aphrodite say to George, 'How am I going to manage alone with *her* all day?'

'I've taken leave,' says George reassuringly.

Seven years later I ask the same question.

Casting my mind back now over some twenty years, I find that that car ride is the only time I have ever heard Aphrodite show the slightest failure of confidence. And her question was not addressed to me. I did not know it at the time, but the constant presentation of confidence, real or assumed, is a vital part of identity for a person living in an oral culture. Never let your oral guard down; answer a question with a question; always assume that the other person is antagonistic; always strive to win, to best your opponent. 'I fixed him, I told him,' is a satisfied comment often heard in Greece.

I did not realize until later how different it must have been for Aphrodite entering a middle-class suburban home for the first time. The space, the carpeted floors, the bathroom, the kitchen and its appliances, the large gardens front and back with their strange plants and no olive trees or grapevines in sight.

She sat in the garden under the flowering gum, plying her crochet hook, flicking the ends of her headscarf back over her shoulders as the heat rose and bees buzzed. The flies bothered her. She waved them away with irritable gestures; they came back and disturbed the rhythm of her crocheting. 'What creatures are these?' she muttered impatiently. And continued to complain.

I try to make a joke about the great Australian salute. She doesn't understand, of course, even though I demonstrate, waving my hand regularly in front of my face. Later, when I visit Greece for the first time, it is the middle of winter; there is no flywire to be seen and flies are always inside the kitchen, crawling on every surface. It is my turn to comment.

'I thought there were no flies here! Why were flies such a surprise in Australia?'

'They were outside.'

'I don't follow.'

She fixes me with a level gaze and says coolly, 'That means they're stupid, Australian flies. Greek flies have brains: they go inside. Always.'

In Melbourne Aphrodite discovers television, but cannot be convinced of any past or future connected with it. Everything and anything is happening here and now, and what happens to all the dead people in the *cow-boyika*? It is puzzling to her that she cannot understand what these invaders of the living-room are saying, for she cannot grasp that there are other languages besides Greek, but she does not worry about it unduly. This is the way oral people are. For literate people a book or writing preserves the moment, as do, now, video and audio tapes. For oral people the memory registers, records, recognizes and recalls the moment.

It was not until 1853 that the *New England Journal of Education* coined the term 'literacy'. Highly literate people cannot imagine a world without books, a world without the search, discovery and discipline of writing. But now, say Illich and Sanders, such people are chained to their own literacy. Yet in Aphrodite's village there are children who do not know that a stamp is to be moistened before it is stuck on the envelope. I know: I hear the postmaster giving them orders and see their bewilderment. They have never posted a letter before.

When television finally comes to Aphrodite's house her old eyes turn from the set to meet mine, and she says, 'Who are these people in here who don't speak Greek?'

'They're from all over the place, remember? From *Ameriki*, from *Anglia*, from *Gallia*, from everywhere. That's why you can't understand them. I can't understand lots of them, either.' But I have the subtitles, for better or for worse.

'Oh yes, now I remember. You've told me that before.'

While Aeschylus stated that 'all arts that mortals have came from Prometheus', Zeus punished him for bringing the alphabet to mankind, for script imprisons, memory flows. Mere mortals should have been content with memory, but wanted more.

Anaïs Nin on writing: 'Almost every other occupation gives more pleasure: cooking, sewing, gardening, swimming, but none of them gives you back the life which is flowing away from us every minute.'

So that oral people often have a quite misplaced sense of trust in the power of the written word.

'Why must we die?'
'I don't know, Zorba.'
'You don't know . . . then what are all those old books that you read? Why do you read? If the books don't tell you that, what do they tell you?'

131

'They tell me of the despair of men who cannot answer your question.'

The Life and Chequered Career
of Alexis Zorba
Nikos Kazantzakis

We go, Yiayia, Dimitri and I, to a park. It is a hot day and we sink gratefully under a shady tree. Dimitri, aged fifteen months and already very gregarious, starts to play with some other small children. They are older than he is and talking rapidly and at great length. Suddenly Yiayia looks at me with an unspoken question in her eyes and then turns again towards the children. After a minute or two she can contain herself no longer and says, 'Those children aren't speaking Greek.'

'Um, no.'

'Why not?'

'Well, they're not Greek children, are they? They're Australians.'

'*Ti les.* You don't say. So Australians don't speak Greek?'

'Not as a rule.'

'*Po. Po.*'

Later she meets our neighbour, who is very anxious to understand and communicate but, as a sixty-year-old monoglot Australian, is quite unable to do so. Yiayia speaks to her and Nor-nor does not understand. Yiayia, completely forgetting the incident in the park, cannot believe that she has failed to make a connection and so roars the question and comment all over again. Nothing happens.

The three of us travel all over Melbourne, from Mt Dandenong to Edithvale, from Emu Bottom to Ripponlea, from the zoo to the Healesville sanctuary, from the Myer Music Bowl to Como. At Edithvale beach she kilts up her black skirts, adjusts her headscarf against the summer breeze, and takes Dimitri paddling. At the Healesville sanctuary she scares me by calmly walking up to a large kangaroo and lifting its tail off the ground. She inspects it closely, the kangaroo inspects her, I hold my breath. Nothing happens: the kangaroo realizes that a harmless scientific inquiry is being conducted. Emus tower over her and fix her with their basilisk gaze, but she flinches not at all.

At Emu Bottom, the restored homestead listed by the National Trust, she is fascinated by her first sight of merino sheep, incredulous at the depth, richness and crinkliness of their fleece.

'What creatures! What wool! What knitting yarn that must make.'

She eats a sandwich for the first time in her life but she does not enjoy the experience: peculiar foreign food, and can this really be bread? Neither does she enjoy her trip to the south-west coast, with its boiling, threatening sea, its wild rocks, and its isolation. George has a boating accident which so terrifies her that she never refers to it again.

But in general she does not comment and I become irritable. Please react, I say to myself, say something, dammit! It takes me years to learn that oral people deliberately do not react. Do not praise, do not give the other party the advantage, do not put yourself in their power by expressing admiration. Do not tempt the Eye. Keep yourself to yourself when you are in the subordinate position. Do not even express curiosity. If you have a question, try to find the answer – lift the kangaroo's tail – by yourself.

And it is not until two years later, visiting Greece for the first time, that I comprehend that the whole Australian environment is something undreamed of, completely alien, and that Aphrodite's stay here has put a great strain on her imagination. I realize, then, all my limitations, for I have attempted to visualize her life, her house, her village, her setting, and have failed dismally. I have my turn at being overwhelmed, at feeling a dislocation in time and space, at going through an experience I have tried to imagine but never anticipated. Words often fail, and sometimes it is better to accept this rather than try to describe a life and a setting that will not be described.

Australia in the early seventies. Twenty years later it seems like a golden era. We had the It's Time campaign and, at long last, a change of government. George and I wrangled over politics; he voted Liberal, I Labor. Gough Whitlam was, and is, one of my heroes, bestriding our known world like a colossus, both literally and metaphorically, oozing intelligence at every pore. Change was in the air: for women, in the arts. We were out of Vietnam at last and my mother could stop worrying about the approach of her only son's twentieth birthday. Looking back through a haze of memory, trying to recall what it was like, I feel that there had been, then, a particular lightness in the air. And I wonder if Aphrodite ever felt it, this contrast between a country where tanks rolled outside the universities and one where people took to the streets in vast numbers, voicing a protest calmly, with deep conviction and in complete safety. That is the way it all seems now. The events of November 11, 1975 had yet to cast their long, deep shadow.

At the same time events in Greece were darkening.

Dimitri's christening. Yiayia is to stand godmother. I have been to Orthodox christenings before, and feel sick with dread. Dimitri has had water-proofing and drown-proofing sessions, all the rage in middle-class suburbia then, and I still do not know whether they were, or are, a good idea. Yiayia knows: she is horrified at the sight of toddlers being thrown into a swimming-pool. She cannot swim herself, and here are these poor babies . . . She is very restrained, however, and says little. Later I realize what an effort this has cost her.

The ritual takes place. Father Nikolaos, the officiating priest, is the one who married us. Yiayia takes the sight of his short hair and clipped beard in her stride, feeling at some level, perhaps, that things are bound to be different in the Diaspora: in Greece, priests have long beards, and their hair, never permitted to be cut, is wound into a bun. Giant chandeliers twinkle, the saints gaze steadily from framed icons, and Dimitri, grandson and great-grandson of Orthodox priests, screams in outrage, fear and rebellion as total immersion takes place three times. Yiayia, draped in white sheets, handles her squirming charge and the whole situation with total calm and dignity. She and he are now linked forever in the sight of God. She dresses him in his new clothes at the start of his spiritual life.

And what else? The party afterwards, where there is no dancing because the family is still in mourning, but where Yiayia is the fêted guest nevertheless. Practically everybody transplanted from the village to Melbourne suburbia is there, reminiscing, yearning, trying to capture, through Yiayia's words and her sparkle as a raconteur, something of the flavour they have left behind and for which they still long. The sighs of 'Do you remember?' float on the summer air.

Later, more visits: to Greek friends who try every day

to reproduce village life in a strange environment, and who shower Yiayia with largesse and hospitality. She is an important person, widow of a priest they remember well, who christened most of them. A visit to Moomba, Melbourne's autumn festival. And who knows what Yiayia makes of the art show, of the fun fairs, fireworks and boats lit with fairy lights gliding down the darkened Yarra, of pie and hot-dog stalls, of couples locked in close embrace on the tight green grass of the Alexandra Gardens.

I take her to Como, most graceful of Victoria's colonial mansions, its calm white presence gazing over gardens, fountain, and great sweep of lawn, and there, at last, she reacts. We tread softly on the polished boards, feel the ballroom floor swing ever so slightly on its chains, gaze at the costumes, and finally approach the collection of gold and silver plate. Yiayia almost gasps, her eyes open wide, and she murmurs, «Τι ωραία πράγματα.» 'What beautiful things.' It all comes together then: the representation of extreme wealth, the lure of great beauty, and the domestic, yet grand, opulent, unattainable, splendour of these objects. A village housewife's tray is often a prized possession, or she might have several, with a very good one reserved for feast days and special visitors. Trays, plate, are symbols of hospitality: here, in Como, I like to think, Yiayia had a passing vision of hospitality being dispensed on an impossibly grand scale, without any worry about routine, drudgery or food shortages. It was a village woman's glimpse of heaven.

Aphrodite prepared to make the return journey, saying, 'I must be home for Easter.' She packed and shed tears. She knew that George had opportunities here in Australia that were not available in Greece, but nine years is a long time and she rebelled, I am sure, at the thought of one son, her favourite, so like his father and so beautiful, being so far away. The thought of the distance must have been overwhelming; she had no way of making a connection over such a long way, and it was unlikely that she would be able to visit Australia again. It was as if a thread were about to snap, one that would not be able to be spliced again, and she was afraid.

So was George. I have not seen my own mother every day since I left home at seventeen. It is enough to know that she is around somewhere, going about her daily round in a big city, just a phone call away. For George this thought is not enough. Deprived of his mother's presence at the age of twelve when he was sent away to school, all he wanted was to have her in his life again. If Yiayia had decided to stay in Australia, as she was quite entitled to do under the Whitlam government's policy of family reunion for migrants, she would of course have lived with us. For George his mother was also, naturally, a symbol of home, the past, and a childhood which, no matter how troubled, he remembered with love for that particular sense of the fabric of family.

Back at Tullamarine mother and son weep, George much more than Yiayia. And he weeps at length in the garden at home, while I creep around worriedly, not knowing what to do. While he is grieving, Aphrodite is arriving at Athens airport and making her slow way home to the village, where she does, of course, celebrate Easter, in the April of 1974.

'We study what man has done,' wrote historian R. G. Collingwood, 'to discover what man is; history is an indispensable form of human self-knowledge.' But often that self-knowledge is scarcely bearable. History combines the universal and the particular, fact and fiction, myth and evidence, images and documents, sounds and silence, the human and inhuman, the routine and the spectacle. The Cyprus crisis on May 1974 is an example of what E. H. Carr called the suffering indigenous to history.

Grivas of EOKA died in 1974 and Archbishop Makarios purged his supporters. But later in the year, Makarios himself was deposed by Greek officers of the national guard, by an Enosis extremist, Nikos Sampson, who became president. Makarios fled to Britain. At the request of the Turkish Cypriot leader, Turkey sent troops to the island and took control of the northern part of it, dividing Cyprus along what became known as the Attila line, cutting off approximately one third of Cyprus's total territory.

In reaction, Greece's military regime attempted a mobilization that was the epitome of inefficiency. Within seventy-two hours of the invasion of Cyprus, the almost total isolation of Greece's military regime in the international community was revealed. General Davos, commander of the Third Army Corps, issued an ultimatum to President Ghizikis, demanding a return to civilian rule.

George roamed restlessly about the house, tuning in to the radio and television, reading newspapers, talking to friends, saying, 'The minute the air force reserves send me my papers, I'll be off.'

Aphrodite, Vasso and all the villagers were laying in supplies, making sure that they had the basics, working harder than ever, steeling themselves against what they were sure would be a repetition of an old pattern. They were very surprised when this did not occur, when the pattern altered.

Konstantine Karamanlis returned in triumph in July. He

had been invited back and thus ended his eleven years of self-imposed exile in Paris. Crowds, delirious with delight, thronged the streets of Athens in the hope of seeing him. He formed, with the typically Greek instinct for the dramatic gesture, a new government of national salvation, and immediately ended martial law, press censorship and the ban on political parties. The old regime disappeared almost as quickly as it had come to power, but deep scars remained as a result of its seven-year sway. In this same year of 1974, Karamanlis's New Democracy Party won a decisive majority in the elections. Later the monarchy was rejected in a referendum. In 1975 a new constitution was adopted.

On election days in Greece, which are always Sundays, the sale of alcohol is banned, all military leave is cancelled, and national servicemen are on duty at the polls. They carry rifles with fixed bayonets. In the past, it seems, ballot boxes have on occasion mysteriously disappeared. How much older people like Aphrodite understand of elections, and political processes generally, is difficult to assess. The family is important in politics, as in all other areas of life, and people tend to be guided by family ties when casting their votes: people will change their party affiliation if the son of a popular local figure is standing for parliament, for example.

We fly to Greece for a holiday in December 1975, George, Dimitri, Nikolaos and I. George has been away for more than ten years. I, aged thirty, have never been out of Australia before. Tearful reunions intertwine with a sense of great adventure. I discover the continuity of family, and the way in which public interest obscures private life in Greece. «Που πας;» 'Where are you going?' asks the village priest as I set off, with one child at hand and one in the pusher to discover how far the sealed road goes. I tell him this.

'Why?' he inquires, and I try to say, 'Because it's there,' at which reply he shakes his head in mystification. Yiayia picks over my bags and bundles and wanders into rooms without knocking, as she used to do when she was in Australia: there she made an uninvited inventory of my meagre supply of jewellery while George glared at me and defied me to say a word. I let my indignant gaze drop and meekly said nothing. Attitudes to property, privacy, the individual are all different in rural Greece.

Nikolaos is christened on a freezing, rainy Christmas Day, and I let Yiayia down by failing to kiss the priest's hand. On another day she takes me to a funeral. We have to struggle through ankle-deep mud in order to get to the deceased's house. Suddenly I stand stock-still with fright, almost becoming bogged, as I hear an ear-splitting wail followed by frantic keening. Yiayia turns to me in surprise.

'Whatever is the matter?'

'Nothing,' I mumble, and pull my frozen feet out of the clinging mud.

She shows me how to make *thiples*, those intricate folds and twists of pastry drowned in honey and sprinkled with chopped walnuts, working away all morning with the mixture, a length of fine dowel, and a deep saucepan nearly full of green olive oil. I notice that Greek women do not, as a rule, work alone. Even when Yiayia is technically by herself, she is not in reality, for the house is right on the street, and the life of the street flows into the house and out again. On fine days during the winter months women stand on their balconies and conduct long-range conversations, their voices carrying through the sharp air. When the *thiples* are finished, other women come to admire and eat.

A domestic task, or any task for that matter, is not executed in order to gain self-fulfilment but as a social activity. Any self-fulfilment comes from the praise of enjoyment expressed by the group.

In the evenings Yiayia entertains. Seated on a low stool by the fire, knees apart under her black apron, one hand outstretched with fingers curled around the handle of the poker (this fire is allowed no disobedience), she is transformed into the Aphrodite of years long gone. She sparkles and sighs by turns over her memories as she recalls stirring episodes from the past. She has immense talent, is a theatre troupe of one, keeping her audience enthralled in her Peloponnesian kitchen-as-salon, enacting comedies and dramas, playing several parts, mimicking different voices, exaggerating incidents, expanding the boundaries of small-village life.

Now, fifteen or more years later, as her life draws slowly to its close, she hears those voices that have gone forever, those of her parents, her dead brothers and sisters. They return to her directly, unaltered, the more genuine the older she becomes, as age blurs the intervening years and makes her a child again. When I first knew her, Dimitrios and Joanna were still alive. Now she is the only one left.

Often in the old days, if the fire was behaving itself, she would crochet as she spoke, fingers flashing in the firelight over elaborate doyleys or the rugs she wove out of long streamers of plastic cut from supermarket carry-bags. Round and round the rug grew large, all shiny blue, red and orange.

Poetry in other cultures has many uses that have been largely lost in the English tradition. Somali poetry, for example, is used as a powerful weapon to win friends, to revile enemies, to praise traditional chiefs or modern political leaders. It is also used to broadcast public events.

Yiayia's oral performance, apart from its own validity, has uses as well. She entertains, she tells a story, she demonstrates great skill, for in the way of story-tellers who cannot write their stories down she spins a tale which has no doubling back. It progresses slowly, with some repetition, but without hesitation, for once the listener's attention is broken both speaker and listener are lost. Yet when silence occurs, even breaks out, the moment has great dramatic intensity and emotional impact.

Yiayia processes the past in this way, undergoes catharsis, finds self-fulfilment in the creative act, breaking the barriers of the domestic and the maternal. She also hones her memory, that vital part of every person which takes on particular significance for one who is oral rather than literate: the traitor memory needs to be disciplined, whipped into submission. For, as Ann Cornelisen wrote in *The Flight from Torregreca*, 'If you can't read, you have to have a good memory. Otherwise, what do you think about?'

Even now, when Yiayia's memory is failing, the lines of narrative create dramatic illusion. In her recital of genealogies, it is the additions that are important. There are no analyses. The line goes on and on, branching into filaments and then returning to the main one.

And this performance, like the *mirologia*, is the personal drama. The *mirologia* themselves are highly dramatic and reach back to Andromache's lament over the body of Hector; a skilful lamenter has a finely polished ability to move others. She is also able to summon up, through her powers of recall, intense pain and grief, as well as poignant memories of the departed and their virtues and prowess. In this way memorial services are able to perform their function of catharsis. The lamenter's whole person is involved: gestures and movements of body and hands are very important. Repetition of key images and elements, similes and metaphors, appeals to the dead person, are all part of the pattern. The lamenter mediates between the living and the dead. So, in a sense, does Yiayia in her hearthside performance.

In the Australian Aboriginal Djanggawul song cycle, three spirit beings travel on the path of the rising sun to Arnhem Land and eventually disappear into the sunset. On their way they create the beings of the natural world, the sun, the morning star, the clouds. And with them they bring various objects central to a complex of symbols. One of these is a string, a length of twine into which are worked orange-coloured birds' feathers. It is also referred to in songs as a cluster of living birds, while the red feathers from the breast of the parakeet symbolize the rays of the sun and the red summer sky.

NOTEBOOK, SUMMER 1980

Yiayia plays verbal games with the children.

'Count to ten in French, Yiayia.'

She does so, chuckling with the pleasure of it, for they cannot do this. She goes on to air the words of English her brother Dimitrios taught her on his return from Chicago. She seems to be a perfect mimic.

'A park charp,' she says. «Καλό φαγητό.» 'Good food, a pork chop. Money. Everybody knows that word.' June, an English friend, teaches her to say 'tomorrow' with a flawless BBC accent. Hearing this, accomplished after a very few repetitions, I become convinced that she could, if taught, recite the relevant speech from *Macbeth* perfectly.

❧

We come back to Greece in 1977 and once more in 1980. Greece is slowly recovering from the years of the junta, Australia from the bitterness engendered by Sir John Kerr's dismissal of Gough Whitlam in 1975. Australia is naturally turning more and more towards her Asian neighbours, becoming, with Israel, the most multicultural nation on the face of the earth. Greece, monoglot and monocultural, is about to enter the European Economic Community.

All these goodbyes. Yiayia has been depressed for a week. I come across her in odd corners of the house, snuffling into her handkerchief. On the last morning the suitcases are roped onto the donkey's back and he stands, puffing and stamping, in the courtyard. I do not want to go through more moments like these, as both George and Yiayia look and doubtless feel as if they have been stabbed to the heart, not necessarily with a knife but rather with a slender icicle. We move off, with Vasso and the donkey, to the bus-stop: we hear muffled sobs as we turn the corner.

NOTEBOOK, AUTUMN 1980

Quite by chance, George has found a job, a good job. He comes and goes. He loves the work. Time passes: one Saturday morning we stand in the courtyard. He says, 'Let's stay.' Or perhaps he doesn't say quite that. But he does say, 'What do you think? *Could* we stay?'

I look at him. He is dizzy with joy, transfigured by a happiness I have not seen before. He has come home. I stand very still in the September sun, and quite suddenly, out of nowhere, a chill wind blows. Around my heart, I think later. But I take a deep breath, smile at him and say, 'I suppose we could.'

CHAPTER SIX
LIVING ON

An aged man is but a paltry thing
A tattered coat upon a stick, unless
Soul clap its hands and sing, and louder sing
For every tatter in its mortal dress.
'Sailing to Byzantium', W. B. Yeats

NOTEBOOK, AUTUMN 1980

So we are here, living and adjusting. Yiayia seems to like having the children in the house, and of course she is overjoyed that George is back. That goes without saying. Living and adjusting.

Here in Greece, death and its attendant rituals are part of living. After an Orthodox funeral a body stays in the ground for as short a period as three years, after which exhumation takes place and all the mortal remains are placed in a box in the church charnel-house.

But Yiayia waits until George comes home before she has Papadimitri's body exhumed. I hear vague murmurings about this event, although I do not take too much notice and cannot really make them out, anyway.

The whole family converges on the house one Sunday afternoon, and it soon becomes apparent that a ceremony will take place and that everybody is expected to attend. The thought overwhelms me; I cannot face such an ordeal. Hastily I volunteer to mind the children, my own and George's sister's. They do not need much minding and people stare slightly, but my excuse is accepted, to my very great relief. Everybody else departs.

Time passes and I am doing nothing in particular when Nikos, George's younger brother, dashes hastily through the gate, rushes into the middle part of the house and emerges clutching a crowbar. He disappears as quickly as he has arrived, leaving me gasping: it has not occurred to me that the family members themselves have to break open the grave. I don't know quite what has occurred to me: nothing very much beyond the fact that I can see space is at a premium in the churchyard. But why the need for ceremony? Later, I write to a friend who is, I imagine, well qualified to supply information about this matter. There is never any reply. Later still, I learn something of the superstitions attached to the practice of exhumation: if the flesh is not in a state of decay, then the forces of evil have been at work.

The family returns home and sits about quietly. Yiayia heaves a sigh, and says, 'His head had got small, hadn't it?' and pulls a wry face. I feel sick and

wonder if I could ever possibly bear to see someone
I had loved reduced to that.

The problem of work, a difficult one indeed. Yiayia's
workload was becoming lighter as mine was becoming
heavier. We both had totally different ideas about work,
why we did it and what benefits we derived from it. Here
there was no common ground. After George and I built our
separate establishment, Yiayia would let herself in at my
front door, see me surrounded by books and papers, or
hunched over the typewriter, and sit down beside me.

'Working? Carry on. Don't let me interrupt you.'

She would then launch into conversation, while I cranked
the cogs of my reluctant brain from English to Greek in
order to make at least some contribution. It became clear
to me, very early on, that what I was doing, in her view,
did not constitute work. I was not using my body, walking
long distances and returning home at dusk aching in every
limb. Work to her was an external process, and she would
never have any idea of it being an internal one. I, for my
part, could not understand the satisfaction she gained from
her daily round, which, to my mind, once the novelty had
worn off, seemed repetitive and boring in the extreme.

'More books, more letters,' she would say, eyeing the
bookshelf and the table on which it was always very
difficult to discern more than a square inch of cloth. 'Yes,'
I would mumble, feeling almost as if she had discovered
a hitherto unknown moral failing in my character. I was,
after all, sitting down and therefore resting, perhaps even
being slothful.

I did not live up to her expectations of what a wife,
mother and housewife should be. I could not make

cheese – and still cannot. I did not slave for hours over the stove, in the house, over my embroidery. She would pad into the house bearing tempting morsels for George, for I did not cook chick-pea soup, octopus or *pasto*. But this was not a reciprocal arrangement, for she would always refuse to taste anything I cooked, wrinkling her nose in distaste and announcing that she could not eat anything foreign. It was a long time before I realized that this was yet another ploy in the continuing game of power: never cede an inch, never give satisfaction. And always, always make the other person, your opponent, as it were, in this elaborate performance, feel that he must persuade you. In the Anglo-Saxon culture, for example, 'no' most often means just that. In Greece it usually means 'please persuade me to change my mind'.

So the various techniques of persuasion have regularly to be employed, the flattery, the cajolery, the emphasis on the goodness of the food. Once Yiayia refused to eat a piece of the birthday cake I had made for one of the children. The small celebration over, George simply presented her with a large slice of cake to take home. She left, still protesting. A few minutes later I noticed that she had forgotten her umbrella. I hurried after her with it, opened the outside door, and was more than surprised to see her leaning against the wall of the yard, munching cake. Crumbs sat on her upper lip. We glared at each other, but I walked away thinking that I had won a small victory and that, more, I had added something to my understanding of the power play, of a different mentality, of a competitive spirit.

Yiayia and I approach the world from opposite directions, view it from different angles, and her great gift to me has been precisely that tipping of the balance, the revelation of the difference, the new view. Once, while we were still living in her house, I bought presents for our sons to give to her. I chose things I admired and coveted myself: a beautiful earthenware bowl with a soft ochre glaze and a jug to match. She gave them back to me. 'Take them away,' she said, 'they remind me of the bad old days. I want modern things. Off you go now and buy me something nice in plastic.' It didn't do, either, to wax too soulful about the beauty of the mountains. 'Humph!' she would say. 'If you had walked and worked in them the way I have, you wouldn't think them beautiful at all!'

When she became ill three years ago, I tried to help, making gestures that seemed to me to be appropriate. Thinking her desperate with boredom, I took her magazines, alive with big bright photographs, which she thumbed once. She was suffering from vertigo, so I produced a walking-stick and put a red bow on it, just for fun, but both stick and bow promptly disappeared into one of the house's numerous hiding places. The next purchase was a big pot of pink ruffled azaleas, a riot of colour which I longed to possess, only to have Kyria Alexandra limp into the kitchen and remark, 'What? Flowers? But you're still alive, *Papathia*!'

Sometimes I wonder whether Yiayia knows the word psychology, whether she has heard the word feminism. It seems unlikely. «Επειδή είναι άνδρας.» 'Because he is a man,' she has said so many times in explanation of how men should be treated or why they behave the way they do. Yet there has been little of the submissive female about her. She has tyrannized her sons unmercifully at times, and I have stood by in amazement while she has flirted quite shamelessly with my father. This cross between ritual and play was inevitably limited by difficulties in communication, but both parties enjoyed themselves hugely, nevertheless. My own mother instructed me not to take too much notice of the myth of the downtrodden village woman.

'Yiayia's sons are used to assertive women,' she remarked drily one day. 'You just remember that.'

So the dynamics of our household changed to admit Yiayia as a power, and to welcome Alexander, the only one of our children born in Greece. Alexander has given Yiayia great pleasure. Disappointment caused by the fact that he is not a girl and that therefore her name will sink into oblivion lasted only a very short time. Now she derives great satisfaction from knowing that he was born in Athens and that he looks every inch a Bouras. 'That child,' she often tells me, with more than a touch of complacency, 'is the image of his father. A real Bouras.'

For life holds no greater honour and achievement than this, the upholding of one's good name, being a member of a good family with a long and proud tradition. 'She's a Bourapoula' is Yiayia's means of identifying the female members of this in-group. And indeed the name itself is thought to come from the Albanian word *bour*, which means hero, or strong, brave man.

The routine of Yiayia's existence continued against the backdrop of change in Greece's political life. Andreas Papandreou swept to power in 1981 and formed Greece's first socialist government, which would remain in power for eight years. Controversies about the presence of American bases in Greece, or the negotiation of full status within the European Community were not Yiayia's concern. Neither was the progressive family law act which abolished the custom of the dowry.

In 1982 Yiayia's first great-grandchild was born and was

named Katerina Aphrodite; in 1987 little Vasso was born. Last Easter I took photographs of four generations dancing: Yiayia, George, Alexander and Katerina Aphrodite. The latter is a lively, bossy, dark-haired, black-eyed, olive-skinned beauty, much as Yiayia herself must have been nearly eighty years ago. They danced the *kalamatiano*, the four of them, Yiayia clutching the mandatory handkerchief and laughing with pleasure as she stepped the round sedately, with the little ones hopping and prancing beside her.

The fabric of family and the continuation of the line are the most important considerations now. We put a top storey on the house. The first time I took Yiayia up to see the completed floors and ceilings she was delighted, and admired the whole effect greatly. «Καλόρρίζικο, κυρά μου.» 'Good fortune, my woman! And may your daughters-in-law, the brides, dance beautifully up here!'

'I don't want them up here,' I retorted. 'I'll dance myself, thanks very much.' She did not say anything, but grinned, and I think we both silently acknowledged the desire for continuity, but also a certain natural antagonism towards those who ensure it. I have heard her hold forth on the subject of her other daughters-in-law; no doubt they have heard her express her views about me. None of us is good enough: that is a fact of life which we accept with varying grace, depending on the circumstances of the moment and the state of our tempers.

NOTEBOOK, SUMMER 1986

Like most of us, Yiayia does not cope well with change. And things are changing for her. She knows that. She is getting older, and nothing is or will remain the same. What is more, all the force of her will, which is considerable, has no effect. Her goat, her favourite and her friend, is dying. The animal is slumped on the yard floor; she bleats interminably.

'Whatever is the matter with her?' I ask, as the painful cries go on and on.

'She's got *kokkalitis*,' says Yiayia, grimly.

I gather this is a form of osteoporosis to which goats are subject because of calcium depletion, the result of frequent kidding and almost constant lactation.

There is nothing to be done and Yiayia becomes increasingly agitated. 'She's suffering, really suffering. Listen to her. Her bones are crumbling and there's nothing I can do.'

The full measure of her desperation becomes apparent when George comes to me and says, 'Can you suggest anything?'

'Heavens, what do I know about goats?'

We eventually remember that we have read something about vitamin C being a natural pain reliever. Humans are shockingly helpless when faced with the suffering of animals: anything is worth a try. The poor goat is very happy to lap up vast quantities of vitamin C powder dissolved in water. Nothing can save her, but she does stop bleating. She dies during the night.

The next morning the dead beast is taken away and Yiayia stands at the gate, weeping, and saying over and over again, 'Such a good animal and now she's gone.'

NOTEBOOK, SUMMER 1987

Yiayia has been unusually brusque today. She catches me as I pass by on my way back from the post office.

'Come in and talk to me,' she commands. I do not want to do this: I have a bundle of letters to read, I want to get on with my morning's work, and the breakfast dishes are in the sink. But I obey, as usual, and stay for at least half an hour, chatting of this and that. Yiayia seems very tense, stabbing the crochet hook into her yarn, holding the tool in a vicelike grip.

Later I ask George whether his mother is all right.

'She sold the donkey today.'

'What? Why? She didn't tell me.'

'She knew you'd be upset. But she doesn't really need him any more, and she's right, he'll be better off doing at least some light work.'

It is the end of an era. For at least seventy-five years there has been a donkey in Yiayia's life. When I first came to live in her house I awoke, in a sweat of terror, at four o'clock in the morning to the noise of his braying two floors below. I remember asking what his name was. Yiayia stared at me. 'He hasn't got a name.' This seemed a grave omission to one who knew of Jersey herds numbering ninety, yet all with names like Buttercup and Daisy, who had spent a country childhood surrounded by Spots and Rovers. With striking originality I christened him Donk, and began to pay him a lot of attention. It was not long before he would recognize my approach from quite a distance and begin to bray loudly, raising a quivering upper lip and bestowing a flashing ring-of-confidence smile upon me with great goodwill. He was indeed a lovely animal, and now neither Yiayia nor I will ever see him again.

Then there were the deaths. In the great heatwave of 1987 we all had to attend four funerals in three days, so prolonged and intense was the heat. Joanna, Yiayia's sister, died. She was as old as the century, a frail, fine-boned woman who in her youth had been thought more beautiful than her sister because she was fair. She had been the fortunate one, people said, because she had gone to live in Kalamata.

And deaths kept occurring. Friends, relatives; a sister-in-law of Yiayia's died high up in the original mountain village. And now Uncle Vangeli is dead: another thread is broken, because he was Papadimitri's brother.

NOTEBOOK, WINTER 1992

'Call me Jim,' he said. 'Everybody does.'

'But I'm not everybody,' I replied, 'I'm your mother and I *can't* call you Jim.' Dimitrios is back, after spending eighteen months in Melbourne, the place where he was born.

A mountainous young man stepped out of the bus on that first snowy morning and I found myself engulfed in a mass of very vital statistics.

'G'day, Mum,' he said, Aussie accent carefully in place.

'G'day, Dimitri,' I grinned, really only seeing a little boy somewhere within that huge frame, a little boy more than slightly worried about his funny name. Aged six, living in Melbourne, he had said, not just once, 'Call me Trevor. Or Ian.' In the village, where we settled before his eighth birthday, he was only one of many Dimitris and one of several Dimitrios Bourases.

And Yiayia's brother dies. He, too, was a Dimitrios

154

Bouras. He, too had been a migrant, and also said to speakers of English, 'Call me Jim.' Dimitri said he would come to the funeral.

'I've done a pretty good job of avoiding them so far. This'll be my first.'

I looked for him in the yard of Uncle Jim's house, but he apparently did not want to enter the place where women were wailing and men were shuffling uneasily and chatting quietly while waiting for the priests. Outside he towered above a crowd of men, his stiffly gelled hair a contrast to the small sea of flat caps. Nobody recognized him; they whispered and muttered about him, for in village society everybody must have a place, must belong to somebody.

He caught up with me as the hearse wound its way along the village streets. It was a soft, gentle day for a funeral; even in mid-winter, the jonquils, growing wild, had started to bloom, and the almond trees were misted in white. Dimitri did not notice. Pale and strained with shock, he whispered, 'I don't like this much.'

He did not like the sight of his father and uncles weeping while carrying the open coffin; he did not like the sight of his aunts transformed from smart Athenian career girls into chthonic presences robed in black and sobbing the *mirologia*. Village life and death have a rawness suburbia's never has. Village traditions are harsh teachers; their methods are not child-centred.

I had, I suppose, protected my children, as I had myself been protected. I did not want them to know about death too soon. In village society, however, even the tiniest child may be present at a funeral.

When Yiayia and her brother Jim met for the last time he knew her, to her great relief: for over a year his mind had been travelling the lanes and byways of the past, with the result more often than not that his American English, learned in the Chicago of the twenties and thirties, was as clear and correct as it had ever been. Long ago he told me that after his return to the village he used to lie awake at night speaking English to himself in an effort to retain it. Now at his funeral, his first cousin, ninety-year-old Xenophon, removes his flat cap, stares, sighs and recalls their grandfather, Pappou Yannis, who died in the same house. Somewhere inside it, Pappou Yannis's great-great-granddaughter, aged fifteen months, toddles and lurches about.

At the church the protests of the *mirologia* are replaced by the lone chorister's chant: 'I am the light of the world.' An elder of the church shuffles around handing out small candles. Towards the end of the service, each member of the congregation lights his candle, and then, at the given moment, snuffs it out.

The goodbyes are said and then the coffin is carried slowly to the grave. One priest scatters clods with a shovel; grandchildren crumble and scatter bits of earth; one son breaks down at the graveside and weeps uncontrollably, calling his father back again. But the main cry is «Αντίο, πατέρα – στο καλό. Καλό ταξίδι.» 'Go towards the good. We wish you a good journey.' And then the mourners turn away.

Now Yiayia is in low spirits, without knowing why. She is obviously grief-stricken and mourning for somebody, but I don't think she knows who. Long-dead people walk through her memories and time becomes meaningless, telescoped, expanded, contracted, confused. The family is worried. So are her neighbours.

'She has chosen the way of death,' breathes one.
'May she be in the hands of God,' says another.

There is no escaping the facts and starkness of old age in rural Greece. Life is reduced to basics: faces consist of sags, wrinkles, blotches, the ravages of time and weather. Here there are no modern, blue-rinsed, mink-tipped, rainbow-taloned ladies of uncertain age. Here there are no greying grandfathers steering golf-buggies, going to Rotary meetings, musical afternoons and boy-scout fêtes. Years ago, I saw a white-haired couple blissfully pedalling a tandem along a Northumbrian lane, and saw an old woman flying a kite. Such things do not happen in Greece. Here the old tend to sit about quietly, waiting for the end.

Remembering Hellmut. When we met he was seventy-six, although much more like twenty-six, if energy and variety of interests are yardsticks for measuring age and its capabilities. His soul clapped its hands and sang every day that I knew him, and still is doing so somewhere. Of course he deserved to go to Heaven, but sitting on a cloud and strumming a harp would be far too dull an occupation – not his style.

A mighty reader in German and English, a formidable chess player whose computerized chess set used to boom eerily – detailing moves at all hours of the day and night – and an astute businessman, he loved life. He did all sorts of things. He tended his garden, whistling excerpts from the works of Haydn the while, zoomed around suburban streets and shopping centres in his Volkswagen Beetle, sat peacefully spinning yarn on his spinning-wheel, went horseriding at Mount Buffalo and walking and climbing in the Dolomites.

He was interested in everything: food, photography,

philosophy, politics, economics, religion, human nature. Tender-hearted, with an impish sense of humour, he described himself as being a devout pessimist, but never gave way to the unforgiveable sin of despair. Nor could I ever descry a trace of self-pity in him. His life had had its share, more than its share, of high drama – suffering, loss, and forced migration – yet he always considered that history had treated him kindly, that he had been one of the lucky ones.

And he was a letter writer. But, inevitably, when he was eighty-eight, the last letter arrived. The surname on the envelope was the same, written by the same typewriter, but the news of his death meant that my life was irrevocably changed. There is now not just a gap in my memory of my Antipodean life, but a hole in my European one. The letters had come regularly, pages of crisp comment about Australian politics (bread and circuses, same old story), advice about what to read, pithy phrases in German – always carefully translated – and proud comments on his multi-talented, fascinating family. And then there were the bundles of the *National Geographic* magazines for the children, and the tins of yellow-box honey. Nothing was too much trouble, and now I miss his voice, his example, his absolute dedication to the notion of *living* life, and of making the most of old age.

Other men, here on this side of the world, also part of history, were not able to change their destinies, but tried to farm, to harvest olives, to survive, after many years of blood and war had absorbed their youth. Now they shelter behind the walls of their lives. They puff their way to the *kafeneion* and then sit, worry beads threading and falling through gnarled fingers, for hours at a time. They may play backgammon or a hand of cards, but more often they merely sit over a cup of Greek coffee or an ouzo, watch the passing parade and engage in a desultory discussion of politics. It seems they have capitulated to the twin enemies: time and history.

But there are exceptions to every rule. Barba Yiorgi refuses to give up, fights the enemies, rages against the dying of the light, all in his own way. He winters in Athens, summers in the village. In neither place will he stay at home, but travels hither and yon, anywhere and everywhere, either quickly by bus or very slowly on foot. Last year, in the city, he tripped and fell from the last step of a bus. Walking-stick trapped beneath him, he lay calling and gesticulating feebly while uncaring Athenians surged past in hundreds, ignoring him, perhaps taking him for a charlatan or beggar. Finally, two elderly women hoisted him up and set him on his feet. He still continues to travel.

The villagers say that Barba Yeorgi is eighty-eight. If ever there was a tattered coat upon a stick, he is it. His hands are knobbed with arthritis, his back and bones are bent, his skin is stretched, parchmentlike, over his jutting jaw. A flat cap settles uneasily on his baldness. Sometimes I look at him and see only a skull. But then he smiles and his face changes: he is alive.

'How are you?' I inquire.

'Let's say I'm all right,' he replies, with an apology for not greeting me. 'Didn't know who you were. Don't see too well these days!' And off he shuffles, on one of his many, many walks up the street, where he does a little shopping and talks to his friends. One day I saw him make his first trip up the street at half past seven in the morning and his last at nine in the evening. Back and forth, back and forth he goes all day, while I watch him, heart in my mouth, frightened that he will collapse in the street. Perhaps that is the kind of end he wants. It surely cannot be long now. But until then, his soul is clapping its hands and singing and preparing to sing still louder. Reminding me of Hellmut.

Even the old women, while not attempting anything new, or even dreaming of breaking the routine of a lifetime, have moments when they sparkle, when they cock a snook at convention. A few years ago, Yiayia and Stavroula, her neighbour, took a taxi and went to a *panegyri*, a fair, without telling anyone where they were going. They had never done this before, and have not done it since. But what a time they had, seeing everything, toddling along from stall to stall, holding each other up when they felt tired. They giggled with satisfaction when they arrived home, sitting down to replay their experiences and relive their reactions.

Women who sit on their doorsteps gossiping and crocheting, or bending over their embroidery in the late afternoon light, often seem very old. They look as if they have been in that position forever, frozen in the frame of a picture; hands on thread, needle or crochet hook, set smiles on careworn faces. Often, though, the picture jerks out of its frame into instant animation, sound becoming more important than anything else, as they shriek over a joke or an earthy expression.

Stavroula sits with hands resting on her very ample bosom, below which spreads an even more ample girth. She is eighty-five and has recently been to the doctor.

'That man,' she says, eyes glinting, 'told me that I should have a complete check-up. The very idea! I've never had one, and it's a bit late to start traipsing around from one γιατρός to another. Besides, I'm not going to strip to my knickers for any doctor. They needn't think it. Just imagine. «Οχι εγώ.»

Recently a gypsy has taken to selling her wares in the

village. She pushes a large handcart up the main street and through the lanes. She sells underwear, linen, aprons and towels. One day George hears her call out to an old woman. «Ελα καλέ.» 'Come, my good woman. Three pairs of knickers for a thousand drachmae. A real bargain. You won't get a better offer anywhere.' Automatically the old woman launches herself into the bargaining ritual. «Τι λες.» 'You don't say. That's what you think. Far too expensive.' She pauses. 'Anyway, summer's coming, and who needs knickers then?' The gypsy retires, defeated.

NOTEBOOK, WINTER 1992

My mother's story of Clarice. Clarice lived in the same home for the aged as my grandmother. It was a beautiful place, modern, light, airy, extremely comfortable. We knew nothing about Clarice, except that she was well preserved and very intelligent. One day my mother, visiting, sensed that Clarice was in low spirits.

'Are you all right, Clarice?'

'No, not really.'

'Why?'

'Oh, I've just got the feeling that I'm not putting as much into life as I might be.'

Clarice, Mum discovered later, was ninety-five.

Some time in this month of May, I am not sure when, Yiayia will have her eighty-fourth birthday. I have not seen her in the flesh for four weeks: I drag out the photographs taken three months ago, and stare at them again. I had forgotten that I took so many. And I had forgotten that in one that old air of combat is still there. From this photograph she gazes straight at me, and even in Scotland, at this distance, I feel myself quailing before the power of that gaze, which has seen so much of what I will never see. In the next photograph she has turned away, the moment of confrontation over. And now I think that the camera sees and betrays what the human eye does not want to acknowledge or believe – that that gaze, still momentarily so fierce, has turned away from us forever. There is a note of uncertainty, now, about her voice, her gestures and body language. She does not belong to the present any more, but to the past and to the future, whatever it may hold.

Yiayia told me once, years ago, that she was born in November. But then she lost her identity card and insisted I join her in a feverish hunt for it. She was pleased and relieved when I found it. I glanced at it and said, 'This card says you were born in May, not November.'

'Is that so?' she said indifferently. 'Well, well. How important is it, anyway? Name-days are more important than birthdays. In any case, my mother probably wouldn't have known what day or month it was. She gave birth so many times, *i kapseri*, the poor thing. And the babies kept dying. Being born and dying.'

It was not compulsory to register girls, anyway.

Quite accidentally I come across a magazine profile of Naomi Mitchison, that redoubtable sister of the equally redoubtable J. B. S. Haldane, the nineteenth-century scientist. Aged ninety-three in 1990 she states, in the profile, that dying is quite the most interesting thing that the future holds for her. In fact, she often wakes up at night and wonders if the whole process has started, and also wonders whether she should take notes. This is what she would really like to do.

For she has always written: on the bus, in the London

Library, and on the circle line of the tube as it went round and round – until there were too many passengers on it. With the profile there is a beautiful photograph of her, peering intelligently at the camera, with a half-smile on her richly wrinkled face. Her typewriter is on the table behind her. The interview closes with the simple statement, 'I have so much to do.'

The Western (and Greece is not Western, not European, but rather Levantine, Balkan and Byzantine) industrial middle class is trained, conditioned, brainwashed into thinking that there is something essentially fine about challenging life, about trying to expand it, about filling it with as many activities as possible for as long as possible. But is there not something equally fine in leading a received life, in taking up the thread at the point where your parents stopped their weaving of an age-old pattern and continuing it for them and for yourself? Is there not a kind of nobility in being content within a small circumference? In modern Greek history there have been countless modest lives, innumerable village Hampdens, and their wives must have been even more numerous.

And such women still exist. I think of a woman ten years younger than I; that is, one who has possibly ten and certainly five childbearing years ahead of her. She has six children, is expecting a seventh, and five of her offspring are girls. She leads a traditional life: the olive harvest, the care of the goats, the vegetable garden and her family are her only concerns. Although the Papandreou government abolished the custom of the dowry, it is still very much a part of rural thinking. The young father is doubtless already worried about the prospect of having to provide dowries in the not-too-distant future. The first girl, old before her time at the age of eleven, is rarely seen without a baby on her hip. Within ten years, or even as few as six, the baby on her hip will be her own.

Last October we were driving along a country road, where one minute we were quite alone, the next, as we rounded a bend, the road was choked with people. There must have been three thousand of them, of all ages. They were carrying candles and bags of food, using walking-sticks or long staves, walking steadily, singing, chatting, joking and laughing. An icon was being moved from a neighbouring town, where it had been presiding over a *panegyri* for ten days, back to its home in a mountain monastery. In this seemingly secular day and age, the combination of party atmosphere and religious pilgrimage was infectious. The town and monastery are twenty kilometres apart, and most of this huge throng firmly expected to walk this distance and back again.

The fifteenth of August is the Feast of the Dormition of the Virgin. In the 1990s the faithful still gather at a nearby monastery to venerate a particularly sacred icon of the Panagia. Aphrodite sets out on a donkey ride of four hours in order to do this. She organizes children, bedding, food and drink, for it will be an overnight stay. Yiayia still speaks of these occasions as though they were bright threads of memory which she holds up to the light and examines now and then.

NOTEBOOK, SPRING 1993

I have been away for quite a long time. Gillian/my self is a different person; so is Aphrodite/Yiayia. She is happy, carefree, snapping her fingers and clapping her hands in time to the music on the radio. She doesn't know me and perhaps that is fitting and logical. Now she divides her time between bed and chair. When in the chair she seizes the hem of her dress and never lets it go: her hands move restlessly with the material, up and down, folding, pleating and tucking.

'Somehow she thinks she's weaving,' says Vasso.

There is also a companion in the room.

'I've got a little spirit here beside me in bed,' announces Yiayia, lifting the corner of the blanket. 'Tch. It's gone, just this minute.'

'You're not frightened of it, are you?' I ask.

'Of course not.' The old note of impatience, much weaker, is still there.

'Is it male or female?'

'Female,' she grins, 'and just about to have a baby.'

'Oh.' Weakly. There is nothing to say.

Later, sitting in her chair, she looks at me, puzzled. She has already made it clear, several times, that I am a stranger to her. It's odd how truth emerges, or rather, is laid bare, at the end: I always was a stranger, and I know now that nothing ever altered that.

'Why am I here, then?'

There is a pause. She focusses and announces firmly, 'You've come on a visit to see how we are.'

I sit very still. At this moment it seems certain she has always known that the beginning and the end would consist of visits, even that the intervening years were not much more. She has the knowledge. She is the survivor. Hers is the triumph. Her life does not consist of visits: she has a place, her place, has always had it.

We stare at each other; my gaze drops first, as usual, and I get up to go. In the doorway, I pause, turn and look at her carefully, wondering if I will ever see her again. In one way she seems the same, with her scarf and shapeless dress, her straight brows and intimidating gaze. But I try to imprint her image on my memory because it is essentially different. There is a softness: wisps of hair escape the headscarf, her face is relaxed, and suddenly, as I stand, hesitating, she is smiling at me. And just as suddenly she raises her hand in farewell. «Γεια σου,» she says. 'Your health.'

EPILOGUE

The first woman fears she is getting old. She thinks strange, disturbing thoughts, thoughts she has never had before. She thinks back over her life – she, who has never bothered, who has never had the time to sit and think. Sometimes she realizes she makes mistakes, something which never used to happen. She is ill, weakening ever so slowly, while the other woman, in a strange way, seems to be growing stronger. The first woman loses track: the thread of her memory frays, splits and breaks. She is able, often with great effort, to pick it up and splice it back together again, but she feels, rather than knows, that the joining is clumsily done, that the seam is obvious.

She has, however, given up actual weaving, gave it up long ago with a sigh of relief once the last dowry was complete. But perhaps there was some regret in the relief as well, even if the setting up and threading of the loom used to take a good twelve hours. Not that she ever counted or measured the time. What would have been the point? Some things simply have to be done, and weaving was one of them.

But there had been a pleasure in it, she supposed, a pleasure in seeing the cloth grow, in stopping to check the selvages, making sure they were not unravelling, in deciding how close or loose the weave should be, in choosing the colours for the pattern. There had been pain, too. Sometimes, she admitted to herself, although such admissions were very recent, she had become discontented with the sameness of it all, become frustrated because she had wanted to spend time creating different patterns, had wanted to try something new.

Somewhere she had seen pictures. In other places she had seen bolts of cloth in colours she could never afford, wall-hangings, themselves a picture, and just there, having no real use. She remembers muttering, 'What use are they?' and then waking in the night to the knowledge that perhaps use wasn't everything.

Occasionally, she remembers – yes, she does remember this – her mind would wander, she would feel a flash of she didn't quite know what, except that it was tied closely to feeling that if she wove one more work-a-day sheet, or one more bolt of cloth for petticoats and nightdresses, she would – well, she didn't know what she would do.

And then, of course, the inevitable would happen. It always did if you lost concentration. There it would be:

a great knot sticking fast at the comb, bringing work to a temporary halt, sometimes more than temporary. It didn't pay to dream; far better to let your mind follow the action of the shuttle, back and forth, back and forth, to let it come to the end of a row and then start a new one, letting the thread lengthen, the strings mesh and grow into the cloth. Constant movement is the thing; the pause, the stillness is to be avoided.

But yet the dream is there, and forms itself, she now admits to herself so much later, into a huge carpet, wall-hanging – a tapestry, really. Of course the dream is a temptation, for it involves vision, an attempt to freeze time. Her real world is that of sound, where life and time, winged words, flow by and can never be, should never be, recaptured.

The dream-tapestry is so huge that it is still not finished. It cannot be finished, because it is her life. In the dream she sits, sending the shuttle back and forth, and slowly the people, the places, the colours take shape in front of her, building bit by bit, row upon row.

She likes to imagine the background is silver, not the silver of the church dome but rather the silver of the back of the olive leaf. The ideal would be that green-and-silver flash, that movement so like life and weaving, that endless back and forth. Rather hard to achieve, however: simply alternating rows would not do. Let it go.

Against the background she would have the church, her father a black shape, his stove-pipe hat difficult to execute, but possible. Then her old house and garden, with her mother working, her grandmothers and grandfathers, great-uncles, great-aunts and cousins a shadowy throng in the background. Brothers and sisters in the foreground: Vasili, Niko, Dimitrios, Katerini, Joanna. What about herself? No need for inclusion, really. It is obvious where she fits in. What to do about Niko, who must be dead? Death is easier to cope with than not knowing. Perhaps a broken thread here, instead of the neat edges managed for the others?

And then another priest, bigger this time. Surround him with flowers like the wreaths at his funeral: gold, red, purple, white. Behind him build an iconostasis of her own choosing. Her favourite saints: Dimitrios, George, Nikolaos, and Theodore, gift of God, staring unwinkingly, placid faces gazing from each frame. Then weave the Panagia, All Holy Mother of God, in her coffin, patient face just slightly raised, certain in the knowledge of the Resurrection and the Life. Not like the woman's mother, Panayota, into whose face she weaves as best she can the expression of pain and suffering she remembers so well in spite of the passage of time.

Which brings her to the problem of texture. Surely plain, flat fabric is insufficient for pain, tears, sweat, toil, blood? A crimson satin thread for blood? It will be a long, very bright one, never far away from the foreground. Make the drops of tears and sweat raised somehow. Manage it. Dull colours against the silver-grey will help. Put more threads in to make the texture closer. And the lost babies? How to represent their little lives? Perhaps a tiny olive tree for each one? Or a lily? Yes, a white lily, for what did they ever know of sin and evil?

There must be a road. Wide or narrow? Tapering, perhaps, because now she herself seems to be the only one on it, wandering along alone after journeys both expected and unexpected. She has not had her parents' life, although they did their best to ensure that her life would be theirs, almost sketching out the cartoon, trying to ensure that the strings and threads would be taut and even. There had been many more knots than they had anticipated. On this long path work in the texture and colour of fear, loneliness and farewell.

But make the grandchildren line the road, all thirteen of them. It no longer matters about the missing grand-daughter, the one who should have borne her name. Put the three half-foreign grandsons slightly to one side, with their father, who, Glory be to God, came back. That had been something unexpected.

And then keep weaving the road. That seems to be the only thing to do. Crochet is a poor substitute and she is sick of it.

A strange sensation, that of time stopping and starting, of sleeping, waking, general dizziness, of a thread fraying and hanging. Not just a thread, really, but a vital rope, like one for the bucket on a well. Let that snap, and see what happens. She is ill, then. She thought so.

'Yiayia. Yiayia.' She drags her eyes open. She has, all her life, preferred listening and talking to looking and seeing, but now sight and vision seem to be important. And the words are odd, spoken by a mature voice which has a foreign accent. She focusses on the face, and knows she should know it. A small hand, softer than her own, is moving gently on her wrist.

'It's all right, Yiayia. I'm here.'

And suddenly she realizes who it is: it is the foreigner who stayed on, the one who knows nothing, the one who looks in the mirror, reads books and scribbles with a pen instead of using a crochet hook.

She draws a deep breath; she really feels quite odd. Not frightened, though. That's one good thing, Glory be to God. She's been frightened so often and has never become used to it. Her eyes are open and she gazes steadily into a pair of brown ones. Not brown exactly, more green-brown, the colour of mud, poor girl. The old woman cackles to herself with the complacency of one who has once been beautiful.

The younger woman smiles back. Their eyes lock. This has often happened before and has not been a pleasant experience for either of them. But then something peculiar happens to the older woman: a shift in perception, a dislocation, a grinding of dimensions; she could not possibly describe it. She does not have the words for such a task.

But what happens is this: she looks into those brown eyes. The brown eyes, for the first time, are a mirror: the older woman sees herself clearly in them, clearly and easily. And it is a deeply strange thing, but in that moment of seeing herself she knows that her carpet, her tapestry, wall-hanging, whatever it is, has been woven. She also knows that it is of little importance whether it is useful or not. Usefulness is another matter. The work has been done, even if not as she would have done it herself, and somehow all those troublesome knots have been untied and smoothed out. Not by her expert hand, but one cannot have everything. The small hand is still moving gently on her wrist. She touches it, but still looks deep into the mirror. And now, at last, she can let the rope snap, let the final string go.

SELECT BIBLIOGRAPHY

Carr, E.H., *What is History?*, Vintage, New York, 1961.

Clogg, Richard, *A Short History of Modern Greece*, Cambridge University Press, Cambridge, 1980.

Cornelisen, Ann, *The Flight from Torregreca: Strangers and Pilgrims*, Macmillan, London, 1980.

Davies, Robertson, *The Lyre of Orpheus*, Viking, London, 1988.

Dubitsch, Jill (ed), *Gender and Power in Rural Greece*, Princeton, 1986.

173

Finnegan, Ruth (ed), *The Penguin Book of Oral Poetry*, Penguin, London, 1973.

Hadjipateras, Costas N. and Fafalios, Maria S., *Crete 1941 Eyewitnessed*, Efstathiadis Group, Anixi Attikis, 1989.

The Hamlyn Concise Dictionary of Greek and Roman Mythology, Paul Hamlyn, London, 1978.

Holden, David, *Greece Without Columns*, Faber, London, 1972.

Illich, Ivan, and Sanders, Barry, *ABC: The Alphabetization of the Popular Mind*, Penguin, London, 1989.

Kazantzakis, Nikos, *The Life and Chequered Career of Alexis Zorba*, Eleni Katzantsakis, Athens.

Lively, Penelope, *Moon Tiger*, Andre Deutsch, London, 1987.

Nin, Anaïs, *The Diary of Anaïs Nin*, vols. 1–6, Harcourt Brace Jovanovich, New York and London, 1966.

Ong, W.J., *Interfaces of the Word*, Cornell University Press, Ithaca and London, 1977.

— *Orality and Literacy: The Technologizing of the Word*, Metheun, London, 1982.

Stone, Brian (ed), *Medieval English Verse*, Penguin, London, 1966.

ALSO BY GILLIAN BOURAS

A FOREIGN WIFE

Gillian Bouras is an Australian married to a Greek. From the ambiguous position of a foreign wife, she writes of life in a Greek village. Her fellow villagers regard her, the migrant in their midst, as something of a curiosity. They, in turn, are the source of both her admiration and her perplexity.

In 1969 we bravely organised two weddings. An Orthodox ceremony was then a legal requirement of the Greek State, but I wanted some English spoken over me as well. The first service passed in a sort of blur . . . A short time later I walked down a familiar fleur-de-lis carpet towards a Presbyterian minister who welded familiar words and music into a brief service of blessing. It was George's turn to be confused.

ALSO BY GILLIAN BOURAS

A FAIR EXCHANGE

When Gillian Bouras, bestselling author of *A Foreign Wife*, went to live in a Greek village for a few months in 1980 she never imagined she would still be there ten years later. In *A Fair Exchange* she further explores the upheavals and pleasures of exchanging one home for another. Out of her experience has grown a love of words and the patterns they make in her life; and despite her nostalgia for Australia, she cannot resist the impact of foreign landscapes and the people that surround her.

WRITERS DEFILED

Fiona Capp

When the spy puts pen to paper there is no telling where fact ends and fiction begins. Security's obsession with Australian authors and intellectuals for over half a century has, until now, remained almost unknown.

Fiona Capp's *Writers Defiled* reveals both the farcical and serious sides of this drama. It is not a conventional history of the ASIO files but a fascinating analysis of the world Security created. In these seemingly bureaucratic documents we find the language of the biography, the critical essay, the social-realist novel, the popular romance and, of course, the spy story.

AUSTRALIAN CHILDHOOD: AN ANTHOLOGY
Edited by Gwyn Dow and June Factor

Australian Childhood: An Anthology celebrates the wide range of writing about childhood in Australia. With knowledge, sensitivity and an eye for significant detail, the editors have brought together scraps from unpublished memoirs, outbursts from administrators, and extracts from oral histories, autobiographies and fiction. Authors include well-known names such as Mary Gilmore, Henry Lawson, Martin Boyd, Henry Handel Richardson and Frank Moorhouse, as well as many who are unpublished and unknown. It is a book which provides unexpected connections for the scholarly reader and rewards dipping into and browsing through. This rich collection speaks to the child in us all.